Unleash Her: Unveiled

Copyright © 2021 Domonique Peele, Unleash Her: Unveiled

All rights reserved. No part of this publication may be reproduced, distributed, or transmitted in any form or by any means, including photocopying, recording, or other electronic or mechanical methods, without the prior written permission of the publisher, except in the case of brief quotations embodied in critical reviews and certain other noncommercial uses permitted by copyright law. For permission requests, write to the publisher, addressed "Attention: Permissions Coordinator," at the address below.

Contribution by Kiyanni Bryan, Write It Out Publishing LLC in the United States of America.

Author: Domonique Peele

Illustrator: Maurice Rogers

Editor: Tamira K. Butler-Likely

Editor: Katherine A. Young

ISBN: 978-1-7377484-1-0

First Printing, 2021

Domonique Peele

unleashherkingdomsound@gmail.com

https://unleashherkingdomsound.godaddysites.com

Unleash Her: Unveiled

By

Domonique Peele

Write It Out Publishing LLC

Dedication:

To my grandaddy, Julius Nathaniel Bagwell, who didn't have the chance to read this book but played the biggest part in my love for reading, writing, and education, and always asked this one question growing up that I never knew how to answer but now have the answer to: "What are you going to do with your life once you turn 18?" Well, here I am now at almost 30, following God's lead and pursuing purpose. I know you would've been proud! Thank you for always pushing me to excel in greatness.

My grandmothers, Shelia and Bettie, thanks for always loving me, supporting me, and being my biggest cheerleaders growing up and even now, but most importantly, thank you for always being in my corner in prayer. There's nothing like a grandmother's prayers and watching them come to manifestation. I love you both. Thank you both for always being in my corner and pushing me to be the best version of me I can be. Mom (Juanita Peele) and Dad (William Peele), I love you! I simply pray every day to make y'all proud and let you see that all of your advice and even the lectures were never in vain. Thank you for pushing me to always pursue my dreams and go the extra mile in all I do. Thank you for supporting me in all of my endeavors, believing in me, and showing your presence and support.

To the Bagwell/Peele family (two brothers: William Bagwell and Devonte Bagwell, my cousins, aunts, and uncles), I love you all, and thank you for your constant support and encouragement.

ANWA-VA (Formerly known as Transformation Church) Family: I truly thank God for allowing me to be planted in this church and receive not only healing and deliverance but through much prayer and prophetic words, and language for my life. I was able to literally find family, discover my purpose, and I'm now able to go out into the world and make a change.

To my hand-picked Godsends (Aresia, Brianna, Courtney, and Ebony), thank you for being there from the start, for pushing me on this journey, even on the rough nights where I had to phone a friend, listening to my ideas, and not just listening but covering them in prayer and supporting them. Thank you for being my accountability partners to walk in my God-given purpose and no longer allowing me to be the background player or sleep on myself and what God has placed inside of me.

My mentor, Chavon Thomas, thank you for your love and support on this journey, for checking in on me often and helping me to remain on track with my goals. Thank you for pouring into me, praying for me, and for leading and setting a great example for me, as well as helping me to birth what God gave me to birth.

You: To the one who God led to pick up this book. God knew that there was something here for you. Thank you for being my why, the reason that I endured what I endured and wasn't able to quit, but rather, overcame to tell you how I overcame and help you find healing, breakthrough, and deliverance in the different areas of your life. Thank you for being the reason that God wouldn't stop using other vessels to call me out of the grave, cave, and cage, because you would one day need me. Thank you for waiting patiently for my arrival and allowing me to be an answer to your prayers. I love you and pray that this book not only blesses you but brings about change for you and all those connected to you.

Table of Contents

Dedication: vi
Introduction: xii
Anchored 1
Anointed 4
Apple of God's Eye 7
Beautifully Broken 10
Blazing Arrow 13
Bride 16
Bridge 19
Clay 22
Choice 26
Companion 30
Complete 34
Covered 37
Crowned in Royalty 40
Daughter 43
Daring Risk Taker 46
Evolving 50
Fearless 53
Favored 56
Forgiven 59
Finisher 62
Garden 65

Giant Slayer 68

Glass Shatterer 71

Glow Stick 74

Healed 76

Heavy Weight 79

Helping Hand 81

Hot Girl 84

Influencer 87

Intended 89

Jesus Girl 92

Kingdom Focused 95

Lavished in Love 97

Misfit 100

Mediator 103

Motivator 106

Number One 108

Nurturing 111

Orator 114

Poised with Tenacity 116

Quality 119

Quiet Storm 122

Resilient 125

Resourceful 127

Sheltered 130

Surrounded 133

Tomb Raider 136

Torch Carrier 139

Unlabeled 142

Unleashed 145

Vulnerable 148

Worshipper 151

Xylophone 153

You 155

Zesty 158

Introduction:

God revealed me to me. He used every bit of my insecurities, doubts, fears, flaws, and hopelessness to help me remove the mask and become the woman you see or are reading about today. God has a way of using the very things the enemy tries to use to destroy us, to help us tap into the power within us and bring glory to His name. He showed me beyond the mask a woman who was bold, confident, called, free, redeemed, powerful, anointed, and loved. He showed me that it was now safe to remove the mask and be free and walk boldly in my truth of who He created me to be as His original design. The things I once let define me could no longer define me or box me in. I no longer submitted to the false labels. I went through a process of unbecoming to become. God reminded me that it was time for everything that had attached itself to me, everything that held me down or tried to hold me back, had to unleash me. I pray that every sister who picks up this book knows that it's time for them to be unleashed too. This book is meant to bring about change, healing, deliverance, and breakthrough to the heart, mind, and identity of every woman struggling like I once did. It's your time to finally step up and see yourself the way God sees you and operate as a Daughter of the King.

Anchored

"He is like a tree planted by water, that sends out its roots by the stream, and does not fear when heat comes, for its leaves remain green, and is not anxious in the year of drought, for it does not cease to bear fruit."–Jeremiah 17:8 ESV

This year, this word definitely hit different after the last few years of my life. It seemed like everything that I had known and in fact unknowingly grown comfortable in was shaken up. I lost my grandfather and uncle, jobs, had to give up my apartment, lost relationships, finances were in shambles… it was almost like rough patch after rough patch. When these things started occurring, I began to doubt if I was walking in relationship with God or if I was doing something wrong, but God showed me that it had nothing to do with that. Just like His servant, Job, God was allowing me to be tested and tried to be anchored in Him, and during this time I came to realize the truth of the matter as the same with Job: the enemy wasn't allowed to do more to me than God allowed. God wanted to prove to me that if everything else in my life is lost or taken away, then at the end of the day, I still have Him and my faith. Another thing that I didn't lose but had to fight for was my joy. I had to learn to get out of my feelings, as we would say, and find my hope and joy in Him, holding on to a *no matter what, it is well* attitude. The year 2020 came in and put the icing on the cake for the word *anchored*. It shook up not only my world but the lives of many around the world. It wasn't all bad, but it surely brought out a lot of revelation and changes, both internal and external. The main one being that a pandemic hit that literally snatched us all out of church abruptly. I grew up in church my whole life, and I didn't know how to survive without it. God showed me how to literally get anchored and pulled me to the mountainside with Him. He strengthened my devotion and prayer life, which I unknowingly was operating in the comfort zone of "I thought I had arrived and everything was going good"; when in fact, God was calling me deeper and deeper. He increased my prayer life. I literally never knew that I could pray like I do. If you would've even asked me to pray before, I probably would've declined or said a prayer to myself. God showed me again that this could all be here one day and gone the next, but what will always remain is my hope and faith in Him. The enemy studies us and learns the weaknesses to play on. He is always after the fact that we are anchored and is trying to uproot us, getting us to denounce God and quit our faith, but we must remain with the declaration in our hearts and minds that it is well and that we will remain planted in Him regardless of what comes and what goes. Material things can be replaced; God can even replace them with better. As we see with Job, God even restores double-fold. If you are experiencing a season of consecutive loss like I did, please know and understand that it shall be followed by a season of consecutive wins if you'll allow yourself to be planted and anchored in Him, even through tests and trials. It is sometimes easier said than done, but with intentionality, it can be done.

Prayer: Father, thank you for seeing me where I am and meeting me there. Thank you for the increase that is taking place even in the midst of loss. God, just as you did for Job, thank you for stripping me just to rebuild me up and restoring to me double for all of my sorrow. Thank you that nothing shall ever be wasted when it comes to you, but you will use it all for your glory. Teach me to lean not into my own understanding as your word says in Proverbs 3, and allow my focus to never shift from you just because the winds blow and the rain comes. Show me that I am anchored and planted in you no matter what. When things happen that are out of my control, teach me to pray and praise my way through. Let me run to you and tap deeper into the place of worship, prayer, and devotion and not retreat to cope with other mechanisms that I feel temporarily easing my pain to keep me comforted. Let the stretching keep me and bring me closer to you, not pull me away from you. Thank you for reminding me that you are a restorer and rewarder as I remain diligent in you. Shake the room, Father, and remove what's not like you so that you can move how you want to move. Continue to mold me, shape me, and prune me for my next level. Let me find ease in letting go of the things you want me to release to you. When the enemy whispers lies, let me not believe them or feed into them, but show me what part of the Word to throw right back at him as it pertains to my circumstance. Thank you for reminding me that you love me and that no matter what, I'll never lose my trust, faith, and love for you, because there is absolutely nothing that can separate me from you and your love including my circumstances. And I will remain confident in knowing that the testing and trying is producing character and strengthening my faith. Amen.

Anointed

"The spirit of the sovereign Lord is upon me, for the Lord has anointed me to bring good news to the poor; He has sent me to comfort the brokenhearted, and to proclaim that captives will be released, and prisoners will be freed."–Isaiah 61:1 NLT

Have you ever felt like you were in this place of confusion concerning your purpose and what God called you to do? You ever found yourself writing sad and angry letters to God with tears dropping on the page, frustrated and simply wanting to hear a loud audible voice from God? No? Well, funny thing is, this was my story. I spent a lot of days sad, angry, and confused, overcomplicating purpose and trying to figure out what God anointed and called me to do. I was in an extremely low place, feeling like my life was going in cycles and the attacks from the enemy were intensifying over me in all areas of my life physically, spiritually, mentally, financially, and emotionally. *Cues the bell* This was a warning sign in itself that I was anointed and that what was on the inside of me bubbling up and being stirred up to come out was in fact under attack because the enemy was afraid to allow that anointing to be stirred up and operated in. I became so fed up one day that I decided to use the practical tools offered in the Word to combat everything I was feeling. The Word tells us in Matthew 17, some things only come by praying and fasting. I decided to go on a three-day fast for clarity, direction, and instruction. During this three-day fast, I drank only water and spent more time being strategic about my prayer and devotion time, where I'd usually be doing something else. Days 1 and 2 were calm and God did a lot of internal work, bringing things to the forefront for me, and on day 3, it was as if God made it super clear yet very vague. He dropped Isaiah 61 on me and at first, I didn't understand why He wanted me to keep reading this passage, but the more times I began to read it, the scales began to fall off my eyes. *Cues the bell again* God confirmed that there was an anointing on my life and there were some things I was anointed to do. Something that I quickly learned over time was to never become complacent, because the task may change; never become too comfortable and excited about positions, platforms, and titles, because they, too, may change; and lastly, never hold on too tight to my own agenda, because God can change that as well. Though all of this was the case, I learned that the anointing is and always will be there as long as I stay at the Father's feet and remain obedient and in alignment with His will for my life. In each season that He has me in, the grace and anointing will flow. I encourage you today: if you are searching high and low trying to find out your purpose, rest in God's arms. Let Him show you step-by-step the puzzle that is unfolding every day; just remain confident in knowing that you are anointed and graced to do anything God instructs you to do. You never have to feel unqualified, unequipped, or deem yourself not worthy. You are anointed to do anything that is done in love, obedience, and honor to the Father. Relax, Sis, and just go with God. Remember: when the attacks become intense, it's often the times when you're tapping into what God has for you and who He has called you to be. There's something on the inside of you that the enemy is afraid to allow to be released into the earth, so during this time, lean in even more. Pray, praise, and worship your way through. Don't give in and don't let up on the enemy; keep your foot stomping on his neck. He's a thief and is after that oil, but we won't let him have it. Lastly, remember that the increased warfare and seasons of wilderness produce that oil. Keep being pressed and the oil that will flow from you will tell of all the hell you had to endure to get it. And God wastes nothing, so every drop will be used, every test, trial, tribulation, and loss.

Prayer: Father, today I come to you asking for fresh fire. Reignite the flames that once burned but have been dimmed by life's tests and trials. God, forgive me for trying to retreat when things become hard rather than leaning and depending on you even more. God, when the warfare increases and the pain and pressure intensifies, remind me of who you are and that you are in control. That Satan can't do more to me than you allow. God, thank you for using the things that I experience and have experienced to press the oil out of me. Let every ounce of it be used for your glory. Pour out your spirit upon me. Continue to remind me when I feel inadequate, unequipped, afraid, or deem myself unworthy of spaces and places that cultivate what's down inside of me and allow my oil to run, that I am right where you positioned me and have need of me in the moment, and that I am anointed and graced to do everything that you have called me to do when you've tagged me for the task or assignment. Teach me to shift when you say shift, to go with the flow of your plan. God, I thank you that you will continue to let my fire burn for you. Use me Lord—I am available to you. Fill me up, break my alabaster box, and pour out the oil, Father, and as you do so, remind me that you are breaking me not to punish me, but to use me and bring out what's inside of me. Let me see that it is being done gracefully from a place of love, let others come to know you through me. Use every drop of the anointing from my life to lead others to you. Remind me that no assignment or task is too mundane or even too big or too weighty, but you've got me and will see me through. Amen.

Apple of God's Eye

"Indeed, the very hairs on your head are all numbered. Don't be afraid; you are worth more than many sparrows."– Luke 12:7 NIV

You remember those teen days where you had a crush on someone, or those beginning stages of dating when you first become really interested in someone? What happens? You begin to wonder about all things concerning them. What did they eat? How did they sleep? How are they feeling at different times of the day? They are constantly on your mind. You want to make sure that they are living, breathing, and doing well. Funny story. God does the very same for us. We are the apple of His eye. He cares about every little detail concerning us, even down to the number of hairs on our head. Now, if that isn't love, I don't know what is, especially being that we each lose quite a few strands of hair a day, yet God still has each and every one calculated for each of us. That's a lot of love, care, and concern. God sees us as His prized possession; we are special to Him. He absolutely adores us and cares. Even when others around us don't seem to care, God does. One thing I've learned on this journey is that I won't always be everyone's preference, but one thing is for certain, I am and will always remain the apple of God's eye. He sees me. He knows me by name. He provides for me to make sure that I have the best of the best when it comes to Him. For me, He'll go to war, even if no one else will. It took me a while to come to this resolve because for years, I struggled with my identity of being seen as the apple of someone's eye, feeling special, wanted, loved, and cared about. I allowed the sting of rejection and abandonment, which took root during childhood, to snatch my ability to see and accept that I was actually the apple of God's eye. God reminded me simply that He takes delight in me and every little thing concerning me. In my high seasons and in my low seasons, He's there and He cares. Baby girl, might I suggest to you today to rest in that knowing that you, too, are the apple of God's eye, no matter who looks at you and doesn't see your worth or your value. Some people will mistreat you, disown you, struggle to see and acknowledge your worth or even accept you, but no matter who writes you off or even discredits who you are and what God has called you to be, God has and always will deem you the apple of His eye. God delights in you. You hold some value and God knows and treasures that. You are and forever will be the apple of God's eye.

Prayer: Father, help me to see myself the way you see me. Help me to push beyond the stings of rejection, hurt, and abandonment and know that you are my Father who sees, knows, and values my existence and the very essence of my being. Teach me to rest in your reassurance that you take delight in me. Let me look in the mirror and begin to see what you see, the woman who is beautiful, chosen, forgiven, redeemed, called, anointed, bold, brave, powerful, and ready to be all you've called me to be. Teach me to hold my head high and keep my standards the same in knowing that when you see me, you see beauty, greatness, perfection in the masterpiece you've created me to be. As I grow to know my worth, let me not let anyone treat me otherwise and those that do, remove the scales from their eyes to see who I am in you. Even if they remain blinded, God, help me to never lose sight of you and who you see me as. Remind me daily that you love, care for, and cherish me, and thank you for your reassurance. Teach me ways to value myself better and become a better woman daily. Continue to heal the wounded and broken parts of me as I get back to the basics and the foundation of discovering and embracing who I am and who you've called me to be. Remind me that I don't need to seek validation and acceptance from others, as you've already died for me and chose me and proven your love and delight in me time and time again. Amen.

𝔅eautifully 𝔅roken

"He heals the brokenhearted and bandages their wounds."–Psalms 147:3 NLT

Often times, we despise the story God gave us or the things that we've gone through and experienced because of guilt, shame, condemnation, or simply not wanting to replay the painful memories, not realizing that those are the very areas that God wants to use as He heals them. He exchanges the hurt and pain in those areas that show battle wounds, scars, cuts, bruises, and scrapes, for the healed version of you that testifies of God performing a Psalms 147:3 miracle. He reveals that healed version of you through those very same, once painful places, yet this time, it speaks from a place of beauty and healing. I was once at an event where we did an activity creating inspirational mirrors, affirming, uplifting, and sharing positive things with and about our sisters in the room. Each person had their own mirror and was allowed to take it home with them at the end of the event. One of my top love languages are words of affirmation, so this activity really brightened my day. Well, that was until one day this mirror that I really loved shattered into pieces, and what I thought for a second was about to become trash turned into God's moment for revelation, and with a little tape and glue, treasure. As I went to pick up this now shattered mirror that laid on my floor in pieces to throw it away, God gave me revelation concerning it. He showed me how the shattered, broken, hurt, and messed up parts of me still held so much value and technically made up who I am today. As I slowly pieced the mirror back together, it revealed that everything was still there; it just had been restructured because of what it had gone through, but it made it even better and even more useful. He reminded me that there are seasons where God will break you, strip you, and peel off layers. He shows you who you are and reminds you that there's beauty in brokenness, no matter what you go through or experience, because it allows opportunity for Him to apply His healing touch and gives Him something to use as you testify and bring His name glory. Regardless of who has counted you out, can't see your value and worth, or thinks you're too broken to be used, remember God has use of you, even with your flaws. And as they say, "broken crayons still color." He allowed the brokenness to take place to get some things in you and some things out of you. You were meant to break on purpose for purpose. This wasn't to harm you but to show you the beauty that lies within you. You don't have to always have it together. God can use whomever He pleases, and He loves the not-so-put-together parts that He can piece together. Those broken masterpieces attract people to Him, at the end of the day.

Prayer: Father, thank you for your reminders of the beauty you find in the most broken parts of my life and story. Allow me to learn to come to you undone, unmasked, and unfiltered, letting my guard down and showing you the real me. Peel back the layers and remove the walls I've built up that have shut you and others out. Use every seemingly ugly yet strategically beautiful part of my life and testimony to reveal your glory and the beauty in who you are and what you're capable of. God, even when the mask shatters, show me to not run and hide or retreat from your presence, but rather run to you, allowing you to cover every part of me. God, I love you and thank you for accepting me, for choosing to still make me the one regardless of my flaws and all. Let me mirror you in the earth. Even when the mirror looks shattered, let your reflection still be one that the people see. Teach me to be me to my fullest, embracing all that I am and being just that. Thank you for breaking me apart gracefully to unbecome what I thought I was meant to be, to be restructured and become what you want me to be and who you want me to be. Amen.

Blazing Arrow

"Then I heard the voice of the Lord saying, Whom shall I send? And who will go for us? And I said 'Here I am Lord. Send me.'"–Isaiah 6:8 NIV

June 2017, God shook up my world and my relationship with Him in the best yet scariest way possible. I had an encounter with Him at the altar at church that I had never experienced in all of my years of ever being in church. Mind you, I was raised in the church, but this particular Sunday, it was personal from start to finish. I wasn't going to church for my parents or for my grandparents or just to wear the cute outfit that I had selected that Saturday, something I am guilty of. It was almost as if Sundays had become picture day for me. This particular Sunday, I was in a place of worship and just trying to get into God's presence. I remember standing at the altar, closing my eyes, and crying out to Him that I wanted to experience the realness of who He was. I wanted an encounter with Him that I had heard about in others' testimonies. He did just that. He gave me an encounter that altered my walk, talk, and relationship with Him, but the biggest takeaway I learned from that experience that day, was that the day God slayed me on the altar wasn't about me, but it was about where He was trying to take me. And that agenda that He had in mind to begin a work in me that day would soon turn into a work through me. This was the start of God's agenda to launch me out as a blazing arrow in the world to spread the gospel to others. I thought it was an instantaneous thing and almost jumped ahead of God to go on a mission trip a few months later, but God brought that plan to a halt. I had heard Him correctly to go and make disciples, but it wasn't yet time. It first began in me, then it started in my home, job, friendships, and now here we are as I type this, preparing to move miles and miles away from home to pursue another degree and work in a field that God has been trying to lead me to. One working in ministry, the call I was running from, but the fire was building up all along and here I am, preparing to launch. The fire that God has placed down inside of you was never about you or meant to be confined or contained. In fact, it was meant to spread and launch. You were meant to launch out into different sectors of the world. While for someone reading this, it may be a sign to go ahead and obey God and make that move boldly in faith, and for someone else, it may mean to stay planted and let Him use you on that job. You're going to need those skills and experience you're gaining for that task over in Africa He is calling you to one day. Remember to let God work in you and through you. Don't skip anything because it can't be one or the other. He must first work in you and then launch you out like a blazing, fiery arrow to work through you.

Prayer: Father, I come to you asking for another encounter with you, one that I've never experienced before. Help me to know you differently and better. God, show me what you've called me to and the arenas and sectors of the world you've called me to. Allow me to trust your guidance and go when you say to go with boldness and confidence, knowing that every move that I make with you will yield good fruit and bring your name glory and honor. Teach me to stay planted when I'm in a season that you are trying to do a work in me. Let me not uproot and move too soon but rather trust and follow your guidance. God, help the fire that you've started in me to be launched into the earth whether it be at work, school, home, or amongst my friends and family. Where you lead, Lord, I'll go, no questions asked. Even when I want to doubt, remind me to trust you and lean on you. Let me walk on water and launch without hesitation. God, show me how to relinquish control and not allow fear of the future, fear of the unknown, and my lack of control of the wheel hold me back from launching out into the deep with you any longer. Teach me to stay in your will and on timing with your plan. Let me not despise or neglect the places you've called me to that are right in front of me in the meantime. Amen.

Bride

"The one marrying you is the one who made you the Lord of heavenly forces is his name. The one redeeming you is the holy one of Israel, the one called the God of all the earth." Isaiah 54: 5 CEB

Stop running from love—something that I had to teach myself. Growing up in a household with rules of no dating until 18 made my love life a little hard, especially when it extended into my adulthood, as I found myself being the almost 30-year-old virgin still waiting on God to make something shake in my love life. When nothing was moving after the age of 18 and I was free from the no dating rules I found myself growing more weary as the years went by. Asking questions like, God, am I not pretty enough? Am I not good enough? Is there truly no one out there for me? Have you called me to be single? Whew, all of these thoughts passed through my head on various occasions. I truly started losing hope in the fact that I'll ever be someone's bride one day. Until one day, God allowed me to come across a sermon called the "Runaway Bride" by one of my favorite speakers, Heather Lindsey. I sat in that room filled with silence in a complete weep and my heart undone before God, as He revealed to me how He had me covered all along and wasn't trying to punish me in the area of my love life. all along, He was simply trying to get my attention and help me to see my identity first as a bride of Christ. I was busy longing for a love to fill a void that only He could fill and was trying hard to fill, but I was running from the true love. God showed me how He was trying to solidify my identity in being His bride before I could ever successfully be anyone else's bride. It's almost scary how content I've become since this realization. I'm sure it will almost take for God to literally tap me on the shoulder and whisper to me that my future husband is "The One." God came in and began to shape my view of relationships and love. He began to remove the layers and knock down walls I put up around my heart, trying to avoid that space of vulnerability and keeping him at a distance. Now it's like He's with me everywhere, talking to me, and I can just feel His love and His presence. He even restored my hope in me being a future bride one day and has given me strategy on how to navigate that relationship when the time comes, and in the meantime, to remain prayerful and in tune with Him, giving Him my all as His bride. I truly believe that God wants the same for all of us, to allow Him to come into our lives and be our number one lover, to show us true love and how to commune with Him. He wants us to use our relationship with Him as a blueprint for our other relationships. If you've experienced some failed relationships, it's ok. Sometimes we fall out of sync with God, but He is the ultimate restorer and redeemer of time. He is an expert at healing and mending broken places. I encourage you to take time to refocus your attention on Him and your role as His bride and allow Him to work through your other relationships and even in your love life. You are a wife and will be a wife. You never have to prove yourself to anyone. God is your bridegroom and will lead your natural groom to you when you least expect it. If you've been running from Him, it's time to stop in your tracks and come home. He's waiting with open arms, just as the Father did in the story of the prodigal son. Don't stay in a place where you identify and become ok with being a runaway. Come home, daughter, your bridegroom is waiting your arrival.

Prayer: Father, thank you for loving me even when I don't take time with you. Forgive me for being on the run from you and your love. Thank you for always keeping your eyes on me and your hand on my life, showing me grace and extending me underserved mercy. Thank you that I begin to see myself as your bride and allow you to love on me and walk like it from this day forward. Father, help me to no longer run and try to fill the void that only you can fill. It was designed for you and you alone, and I thank you for loving me and filling every void in my life. When the enemy tries to distract me, help me to be aware of his tactics and agenda. Show me how to navigate my single season. Help me to steward my single season well and live it full out as your bride. Let me not become weary and discouraged, for you are a God who hears our cries, sees our lonely days and nights, and knows just how to handle us in those moments. Keep me busy and occupied with you and the things you've assigned to me, that I won't waste time in fear that my groom won't find me, because I know in due time, you'll lead him to me and we'll be in divine alignment, and he won't pull me from you. Father, thank you for my married season, that I won't go in with pre notions that my marriage will fail because I've learned to steward relationships and navigate that season as well with your help. Continue to strengthen me in my wait or in my marriage, and show me to love and be loved even in the hard seasons. Restore my hope during the wait, surround me in your love, teach me how to be a better bride before it happens, and even when it's my time, let it flow and let me remain humble, teachable, and keep the fire burning for you and my husband. Thank you for reminding me of who I am as your bride and that nothing can ever separate us, not even death. Amen.

Bridge

"And you will be called the repairer of the breach, The restorer of the streets to dwell in." Isaiah 58: 12 ESV

One Saturday afternoon I was headed to an evangelism event, and I realized I was kind of nervous to go out of fear of not knowing what to tell these random strangers. Or, what could I possibly have to offer to them? I was basically born and raised a church girl and didn't think I'd be able to steer these people to the Father, assuming I would be unrelatable, and in that very moment, God arrested me and showed me that it's not about what I could do in my own strength but rather what He could do through me just because of my obedience and availability in that moment and throughout my encounter with all of these people. Throughout the event, I came to realize in that moment that God showed me it was never about me. He just needed me to be obedient and available to use me as the bridge to get them to Him. Oftentimes, we are just that: we don't have to do much but be somewhere and do and say exactly what God instructs us to, because we are like the middle man of getting them to Him. Sometimes this may be through words, prayers, acts of kindness, being silent but present. While we've all had our own personal experiences and encounters with the Father, one thing remains the same, that we all have a story to tell and something to offer someone out there, even if we can only reach one. That one will then serve as the bridge for someone else. I oftentimes think of the story of David and Saul and am often reminded that all it takes is one. One can chase one thousand and two can chase ten thousand. I began to witness from a place that was genuine and shared my personal salvation story. Sometimes it doesn't even have to be that, but just being an example of love will often lead others to the Father, as well as giving them an encounter with something they've never experienced or may have experienced and possibly turned away from for whatever reason. A bridge is often built for people to cross it, it joins and connects things, and takes us from one location to the next. Without it being in place, many of us would be stuck in transition. This is the same concept with us. God wants to use many of us to restore others back to relationship with Him or lead them to Him for the first time ever. Many of us are called to be the middle man between God and others we just simply have to be present and willing. A living witness of this is Queen Esther in Esther 4:14. Because of her, someone else was able to live and experience new life and without her, they wouldn't be where they are today. Some people have a yearning and longing to be close to the Father and just aren't quite sure where to turn or where to start on doing that, and that's where God sends His children on assignment to step in and stand in the gap to serve as the bridge to accomplish this task. If you go about your day and don't understand some things, just remember this: you're everywhere you are for a reason. Keep showing up, and don't allow the enemy to distract you or deter you from the assignment in which you were placed here to do.

Prayer: Father, thank you for reminding me of the importance of my ability to serve as the bridge in the gap for others to help them navigate this life and find true life in you. Thank you for allowing me to continue to show up and be available to you and allow you to use me to help those who are stuck and lost in transit or those who may have even broken down or turned around on the road and need some redirection.

Continue to give me wisdom, insight, and instruction on how to navigate through the task as a daughter and servant to be the bridge for others to get to you. Father, allow me to know that all I have to do is show up and remain available for you to use me in whatever capacity I am needed in that moment. As I continue to be a part of the bridge ministry, allow me to learn the art of love and have the capacity to serve your people. Show me how to handle every encounter differently. Let it be shaped so unique and strategic that whomever I encounter will know that it was a God-sent thing and a divine encounter with you. Let me never lose sight of the bigger picture but to graciously continue to be in position. Amen.

Clay

"Yet you, Lord, are our Father. We are the clay, you are the potter; we are all the work of your hand."–Isaiah 64:8 NIV

Since the beginning of time God has emphasized his creative and artistic abilities. He still displays them today through us. We are like his artwork on display. God takes us (the clay) and molds us it into something beautiful and puts us in his exhibits for display throughout the world. The most interesting part of it all is that no piece of artwork is that same even if He wanted to duplicate it (hence the existence of twins; they may look alike but there's always something different) No matter how beautiful, fancy, extravagant, or simplistic the artwork may seem we all have to come to realize that there is no accident, mistake, or failure with our creator. He is very strategic when he creates us and allows room for there to be something significant in and about each of us that stands out because He gave us all a special touch. We all belong to the greatest artist to ever exist. After all, He created the earth, sun, moon, and stars. He has been in the business of creating since day one, and we were a part of that plan. We are the work of His hands that He took His time on. God breathed on us and called us good. He liked what He saw, He knew what you'd be like today in this very moment, what you were like in your past, and what you'll be like 10-20 years from now, but guess what? You will forever be beautiful to Him no matter what. He says it in His word Himself, in Psalms 139:14, that we are fearfully and wonderfully made. So the next time you look in the mirror and see disappointment, feel disgust, feel worthless and insignificant or a hot mess, you have to do a reevaluation and remind yourself of not only who you are but whose you are. You are God's

Daughter, His beautiful creation, the work of His hands, and nothing that He makes fails, nothing that He makes is wasted, nothing that He makes is ugly or pointless. You are beautiful artwork. Enjoy being that canvas that God painted, that abstract piece of art that He put His special touch on and now puts on display in His art exhibit in the earth. Lastly, understand even the ashes God can make use of. He gives us beauty for our ashes, so where life has taken its toll on you, let me encourage you that there's beauty in that too. Let the artist work. Relax Let the potter mold you into the beauty He wants you to be. Get comfortable with the thought of who you are becoming in Him. You are a masterpiece and work in progress. Don't let yourself or anyone else talk you out of that, the process of becoming isn't one for the faint but don't quit or grow weary. You are simply on the path of becoming the best version on you that He saw before the foundation of the earth. Lastly, may I suggest that we carry our Father's DNA and are called to create in some capacity throughout the earth. This may look different for us all but there is some artistic ability God has bestowed upon you to build, write, paint, sing, produce, to release some form of color and beauty into the earth. You must now begin to see your worth, tap into those abilities God has given you, and act accordingly. Continue to let God shape you, mold you, and make you into who He saw before the foundation of the earth so that you can release whatever it is He has assigned you to release.

'

Prayer: Father, help me to see me how you do. Thank you for the beauty that you form out of the ashes of my life. Thank you for never allowing anything to go to waste. Father, allow me to look in the mirror and see the beautiful masterpiece that you created. Even at times when I see otherwise, even when others speak differently, or even when I begin to believe differently, allow me to only come into agreement with the thought that I am fearfully and wonderfully made, I am beautiful, and that this beautiful artwork you created is in the hall of fame exhibit for others to see. Thank you for letting me see my difference and embrace it, for allowing me to see my importance and acknowledge it. Help my eyesight to see the "it is good" that you saw when you formed me. Thank you for allowing me to understand that no work of your hands is a failed attempt at creation but rather perfection. Teach me to affirm myself and others around me, that we all may see ourselves as masterpieces and be confident in that and in you. Even now Father I speak to the creative in me and ask that you will continue to lead and guide me in all that I do, say, produce, and release into the earth. May every God-given idea succeed and not lie dormant, be aborted, or fall to the ground. I pray that fear and anxiety will no longer keep me trapped and confined from releasing what it is that you want me to release and when you want me to release don't let me move ahead or behind you but right on time. Remind me to continue to consult you in all that I do let your light shine through me let your power flow through me and show me the black and white areas that need a dose of your color in the earth let me be the light and bring the color. May the ideas that you give me not only be good ideas but game changers for the generations to come. Allow these ideas to break generational curses, change trajectories, shift nations, and even create lasting legacy and generational wealth for those to come after me. May the ideas and gifts that be released through me even outlive me and be helpful to catapult the next generation into even more creative ideas. May nothing I set out to do fail even if it takes many steps and process may it always end well and you be pleased. Amen.

Choice

"In Him we were also chosen, having been predestined according to the plan of Him who works out everything in conformity with the purpose of His will."–Ephesians 1:11 NIV

August 30, 1992 was a day of importance, as it signified my birthday, the day that God allowed me to grace the earth with my presence, reminding myself and others that I am chosen. I was a choice from the day of conception and even before then, God knew that I would be born to two teenage parents who would have a decision on whether I was born, and He allowed me to be here. Although I'm often jokingly reminded that I wasn't planned nor expected, God's word says otherwise. God chose me to live through many dangers seen and unseen. He allowed me to not have to endure being given up for adoption or even aborted. Why? Because I was a choice, a choice that He allowed to live to even write this book today. This may not be your exact story: maybe you don't know your biological parents or didn't get to grow up with them around, maybe you were adopted or almost aborted, but that still wasn't the end for you, and in fact, if you are reading this right now and pause to feel your heartbeat, God made a choice in this very second to make you a choice and candidate to remain here for use. You have a purpose, and God chose you for such a time as this. Oftentimes, people will try to curse our existence and the very essence of our being and remind of us how we are an accident, a mistake, a nobody, or unnecessary, but God reminds us that we are called and we are chosen well before even our parents knew of us. He had every day of your life and my life mapped out. So, cancel those negative words others have told you. I've been listening to a song this week and the singer gets to a part where she sings *You are a miracle*, and I find myself in a weep each time because it again reminded me that I am necessary, important, needed, and predestined to be here. Nothing about me being here right now or even writing this during this very moment is an accident, because God knew that I would be a vessel in this moment to speak to you and remind you that God chose you, sis, and there is absolutely nothing you can do about it. For many reading this, you may have been on the verge of being the one aborted, but God allowed you to live. You may have been diagnosed with an illness no one expected you to survive, but you're here. You may have walked away from that accident that you should've died in; you may have lost everything you had, but you're still here. You may have had to serve that time in prison, but you're still here. You may have been molested or raped, but you're still here. You may have been in a domestic violence relationship, yet you survived and made it out alive. You may have been homeless and alone, but you're still here to testify of it. You may have even attempted suicide or be on the verge of doing so because life has simply gotten too hard, none of you are reading this by accident at this moment. Whatever your story is, I just encourage you to take a look in the mirror and understand that your birthday proved that you were a choice, and today, as you stand in the mirror, proves that you are not only a choice but a miracle, and God chose you to survive and come out alive from some of the hardest battles that some could never endure. As you're reading this, I want you to just envision me hugging you so tight right now and just whispering into your ear that you, my sister, are a choice. God meant for you to be here. If you are on the verge of suicide, know that God loves you and chose you, and you can't give up on that or those attached to you. Everyone won't always choose you—they didn't and some still don't even choose

Jesus—but know that He has people out there who are for you and choose you as well, and I am one of them cheering you on and rooting for you to fix your crown and know that you are chosen. If you didn't get selected for that sorority, job position, house, team, or deal, it's ok. God still calls you qualified and chosen.

Prayer: Father, thank you for never giving up on me or leaving me hanging to die. Thank you for allowing me to survive some of the toughest battles I may ever have to face. Thank you for the strength, peace, stamina, and endurance you give me daily to run my race that was chosen for me and keeping me in the fight, choosing to live. Thank you for helping me to see that miracle that you've made out of me and my life, allowing me to wake each day with air in my lungs, activity in my limbs, and a purpose and destiny, before reminding me to keep my heel on the enemy's neck and not to hang myself by the neck physically or in the spirit. Show me those that are for me and lead me to them. Give me wisdom and discernment on those to keep near. Help me to live each day as if I'm chosen, a miracle, necessary, and the answer to someone else's life so I have to continue to live. Take away suicidal thoughts if they come to plague my mind, and breathe fresh breath and new life into me even when I feel that life has made me grow weak and weary wanting to give up. Let me see and know that there's a light in the darkness and although I am in the pit right now that you are a God who cares for me and will rescue me even at my lowest. Let me see Psalms 27:13. Be my story that I will live to see the goodness of the Lord in the land of the living. Thank you again for choosing me and surrounding me with those who genuinely choose me too. Let me not take offense to those who don't but love on those that do and embrace them. Amen.

Companion

"A person standing alone can be attacked and defeated, but two can stand back to back and conquer. Three are even better, for a triple braided cord is not easily broken."–Ecclesiastes 4:12 NLT

Companionship is often seen in a romantic standpoint but can be attributed to any relationship. For some, you may be in a season of isolation or, like myself, have once experienced it. Don't get me wrong, there are times where God will call you away to the top of the mountain to get away from everyone and everything and spend some much-needed quality time with Him, but the problem comes in when self-sabotage, childhood traumas, and triggers surrounding abandonment and rejection, or fear of the opinion of people begin to show and cause further isolation beyond those God-ordained seasons. As I reflect, I've found that there were times where I pushed people away and shut them out, afraid to allow them in out of fear that they would leave. I began to not trust some out of fear of being vulnerable. I simply began to believe even the personality tests that suggested that I was an introvert and used these things as my escape when in actuality, God was calling me into relationship with others. He was trying to send Godsends and divine connections. Meanwhile I was isolating and self-sabotaging. He was trying to show me that I was built for relationships, friendships, sisterhood, and community. In the background, what I didn't see was the enemy at work to keep me from desiring these things or allowing them to happen for me, because He understood that if He allowed me to experience this then I'd experience more than just that, but I'd also have an encounter with breakthrough, healing, deliverance, and restoration. I'd link up with others and we'd become a force to be reckoned with confidently embracing every part of us and walking out our God-given purpose. The enemy understood that this would ultimately set me up and put me on the path to destiny. There are times where we must be aware that the enemy can also use this tactic to get you alone in a place and tear you apart causing you to experience loneliness, internal conflict, depression, mental anguish and exhaustion, and inner turmoil. This was my story and I understood that isolation was destroying me by the day. It wasn't until one day I reached a point where I was tired of feeling alone and dealing with so many failed relationships that I cried out to God to send me the right people to be surrounded by that could help me to elevate, grow, and become all that He was calling me to be. I prayed for God to surround me with those who had language for my future and even if they seemed more advanced, knowledgeable, and grounded in various areas of life than myself, that I wouldn't shrink back and run from the relationships. We must realize that although we may be good by ourselves, we literally become a force to reckon with when we are in partnership and connection with those God has called us to be in companionship with. There was some challenge in accepting this, as I was once one who dealt with the sting of rejection and abandonment issues, as well as a loss of a sister at the age of five. That loss made me not want sisterhood because I always began to have thoughts and feelings of, God, I wasn't even good enough for you to allow me to experience sisterhood with my only blood sister before being thrown into sisterhood with complete strangers. I literally had to learn to tune out and silence the voices of the enemy that tried to convince me to run and retreat to my cave of isolation and push people away. I had to allow God to work on my heart and let me be planted. I had to learn to love again and allow myself to be loved without feeling threatened or afraid of what being in community would do for me. Today I feel Holy Spirit guiding me to encourage you who are reading this book to never give up hope on community, friendships, divine connections, relationships, and sisterhood, to keep praying through it and being open to receive as you go. Sometimes we just need God to open our eyes to what's in front of us, because we can sometimes miss who He is sending our way. I encourage you to look around and not despise the small beginnings. Even if God has blessed you with one, take that relationship and let it thrive, and lastly, if the enemy has convinced you that you're better alone in isolation and can handle it all on your own, don't live in isolation another day. Come out of the cave, sis. It's a season where God is using connections to launch us and catapult us into our next season and into our destiny more than ever. Get connected.

Prayer: Father, thank you for showing me how much you love me by surrounding me with people who love me like you do. Help me to know how to identify my Godsends and those divine connections that you place in my life and maximize the relationship, letting love grow and flourish. Father, let me learn to let down the walls of my heart and not run out of shame and fear. Strip the layers from around my heart that cause me to shut others out. Allow me to be able to testify of what you've done for me through community. Let me love others back to life as they do the same for me. Father, thank you for allowing me to come out of the cave of isolation, for pulling me up out of a place of loneliness and depression. Revive me in the areas of my life where the enemy has attacked me where I was alone. Where I have experienced loss of relationships, restore those that were prematurely ended. Help me to process through the grief of losing a sister, friend, mentor, or relationship physically, as well help me to not allow that to define me but strengthen me to love harder when you present a second chance. Lastly, thank you for helping me to team up, partner with, and collaborate with every sister I am to connect with and allowing us to be a force to take the kingdom of hell by force through uplifting, encouraging, supporting, and empowering one another in both words and actions. Thank you for letting the longing for sisterhood and connection be fulfilled, and as you stock my life and surround me with other amazing women, teach me to love them, honor them, uphold them in their weakest moments, intercede for them, congratulate them, celebrate with them, be accountable to them, and show up for them and our relationship in the capacity that they need me to. Let the narrative shift for them too and how they see friendship, sisterhood, and community. Give me a keen spirit of discernment to continue to navigate the seasons, times, changes, and dynamics of each relationship I am in so that it remains healthy and productive for your kingdom and forever flows in and with love. Amen.

Complete

"Not that I was ever in need, for what I have learned how to be content with whatever I have." Philippians 4:11 NLT

Have you ever found yourself praying down the Heavens, petitioning God to shift you from one season to the next or one position to the next, not realizing you were discrediting the fact that He has shifted you into a new season or even moved you to a place and position that you once prayed for? Well, I have, and I was good for it. In my life, God has taken me on an extensive single journey, one that I know He'll use for His glory. Growing up, my family had rules of no dating until you were 18. Well, I just knew that at 18 I'd be living that truth, but funny story here, I am at almost 30 and this is still not my truth. At times it would become so frustrating, like, God, why is there such a hold in this area of my life? Recently, God has shifted my perspective on this single season and allowed me to find the joy and contentment in it. I've come to realize that there are lots of things that I am able to do that I wouldn't if I were settled with a family. While, yes, it is a one-day prayer that I hope God fulfills, this season I am in has been a joyous ride. God has done some extensive and miraculous healing in me that I sometimes can't even wrap my mind around. One of the results of it was this book finally being written from a healed place, something that probably wouldn't have happened had I been in another season of my life. I didn't realize that this attitude was slowly making its way to other areas of my life such as work. I was in actuality feigning for titles and positions to fill voids I was overlooking. I thought I wanted these things for one reason and down the line, realized they weren't for me at the time because the season I was in, God wanted to do some stretching and pruning, as He loves to do. If I would've landed in some of the positions and roles I applied for, I would've failed because of character or lack of true interest. This is in no way to discourage you from running for higher positions or even wanting things such as relationships and children, but moreso to remind you to take you and find contentment in whatever season God has you in, because if you strip away every title, label, and thing you find your identity in, then you'll be hurt and stuck, not knowing who you are in Him. Some of the things I was praying for, God did the opposite and stripped me of, but I allowed Him to take me through that process. It was quite uncomfortable but rewarding in now knowing that when people ask who I am, it has nothing to do with a physical title but who God sees me as. God has taught me that I am complete and whole in whatever season and space I am in. I have experienced seasons of having lots of material things, being in great positions, and feeling on top of the world, but I've also experienced other seasons of having to give up everything to follow God and His plan. Nevertheless, God revealed during these times that I am always whole, complete, and to be content where I am. Yes, work hard and go after what you want, but don't define yourself by it or allow your identity to become wrapped up in it, because it can easily be taken away or God can ask you to give it all up. Ask me how I know. You are Whole. You are Complete. Remain content with where God has you and keep the spirit of expectancy for your next, but don't skip the now.

Prayer: Father, teach me to find my wholeness, completeness, and contentment in you and not in the things that I have or the season you have me in, as these things can easily change. Teach me to be grateful in the low seasons and learn what you want me to learn. Teach me to rejoice and be grateful in the high seasons but never forget to keep a lose grip on it. Thank you for the lessons and the blessings in wherever you have me positioned, whether it's my season to sign the house deal or live with a relative or friend, work a 9-5 or my business is booming, be happily married or if I'm as single as a pringle, taking the bus or driving the nice car I prayed for five years ago. God, I thank you for helping my joy and contentment to remain in you. Forgive me of any times where I've been ungrateful and failed to realize that the very thing is before me that I once prayed for, because I now have shifted my sight to wanting to move to the next season. Help me to walk this journey at your pace and never jump ahead of you because of discontentment. Remind me that I lack no good thing in any season I'm in because if it's for me, it'll be in my hands or you'll give me the steps and strategies to obtaining it and reaching it. Thank you for where you have me. I love you and thank you for this daily journey, as it keeps my eyes and faith focused on you. Let me not get out of step with you, but also never allow my faith and spirit of hope and expectancy to waver because of what I don't have or don't see. Let each season and space you place me in be used for your glory as it strengthens me, grows me, and teaches me new things. Amen.

Covered

"He will cover you with His feathers. He will shelter you with His wings. His faithful promises are your armor and protection."–Psalms 91:4 NLT

One day at work, a coworker asked, "If you had one word to describe God, what would you use?" and I said "A cover," but it wasn't until the a few years later I truly learned the meaning of that. And in reading Psalms 91, God gave me revelation of exactly why I felt that way, because He literally is my covering. I am a part of His flock whom He shields, protects, and defends from evil and evil doers. In order to get to me, you literally have to get through Him. The enemy sometimes tries to distract us and negate this truth in our lives and whisper lies that we are alone, lost, wandering, and unprotected. There was a season of my life where I felt that I was under some intense warfare, my mind was under attack, things around me were literally falling to shambles, and I was losing things back to back. I began to believe I was what we'd call an orphan wandering in the field alone while hell was launching its attacks. One of the hardest things of this season was literally seeing the attack come in the form of a person. Whew, was that intense. The more I settled in my identity as an orphan, my attitude changed and my posture changed. I became more defensive, angry, and wanted revenge on those who I felt cut me with their words and betrayed me with their actions. I learned in that season that it isn't necessarily true that words don't hurt, but now I can say that while they hurt in the moment, nothing can ever take me out or harm me because I am covered. Sometimes you may have to go through that season, like myself, where you have to show a mean boss the love of Christ and remain on a prayer assignment when you'd rather leave. You may have to endure a little warfare to allow God to strengthen your prayer life and teach you some prayer strategies. You may have to experience that wilderness for just a little while, but know that you are never, ever alone and that God has you covered. As I type this, I am screaming this loud, to the top of my lungs, to reiterate to you that, sis, YOU ARE NOT AN ORPHAN. God has got you covered. Release those people who hurt you to God, those negative words, those word curses, those painful insults. Love them and remain prayerful through it. Easier said than done, but if you allow God to soften your heart towards them, you'll find peace, strength, and courage to do so. I can testify to this. Most importantly, remember that no hurt, harm, or danger can come your way that God can't cover or protect your from. He's a loving father and doesn't want any harm coming to His children.

Prayer: Father, I come to you today asking you to help my broken heart, the one that feels bruised, wounded, and scarred from the words spoken to me and over me, from enduring seasons of warfare and feeling like I am alone and growing weary. Remind me of your love and how you are my Father who protects me, keeps me, shields me, and covers me from hurt, harm, and danger. Continue to keep me covered. Help me to become anchored in my identity as a daughter, knowing that I am covered and don't have to try to defend or protect myself. Soften my heart and allow me to have the strength, courage, and boldness to love them through it and to love all of the hell out of them when it seems easier to hold a grudge and give up on them. Show me what's a prayer assignment and what's a distraction and trick of the enemy. God, rejuvenate me when I feel weak. Allow me to use the seasons of warfare to be ammunition for other seasons and other assignments. Thank you for the blood that keeps me and protects me. Continue to strengthen my prayer life and give me strategy to navigate each season. Give me the words to say, and show me how to love those who hurt me. As you've shown me that you cover me, teach me to tap into the overseer anointing in me and protect and guide the flock that you've assigned to me in each season of my life. Thank you for placing others in my life to continue to cover me as their sheep. Amen.

Crowned in Royalty

"Yet you made them only a little lower than God and crowned them with glory and honor. You gave them charge of everything you made, putting all things under their authority."– Psalms 8:5-6 NLT

In middle school and high school, I always found myself wanting to run for the various superlative awards and be deemed as the queen of something, but year after year, I counted myself out, thinking that only the popular people would win and be selected, as they always do. I allowed fear to constantly strip me of the opportunity by feeding me lies that I wasn't good enough and didn't belong in anyone's court as a candidate. One day after an event I went to, there were some royal king and queen chairs there and I wanted so badly to finally have a picture in the royal seat. As my photographer took my picture, a bystander walked by and uttered words to me that resonated with the deepest parts of me that they didn't know I needed to hear at the time, and they were very simple but full of meaning. "You look like you belong in that chair." It was the looking like I belonged for me. In my heart I knew that I belonged in that seat both physically and in the spirit but at times, I had trouble believing it and would give that position up to everyone, including the enemy, without a fight. God reminded me that day that He has placed me in that royal seat. I am His kid and an heir to the throne, so that is right where I belong. He reminds us in the word in Hebrews 1:13-14 that your seat is even higher than the angels but most importantly, all of your enemies are at your feet as a footstool; there's absolutely nothing they can do to you. Even they must bow to God. It's important for us to keep this posture and take our seat of authority unapologetically. I know I did that day, and moving forward, something clicked in me. I am a child of THEE King, that's my seat, and I have the right to remain seated in it. There will be times where life tries to throw its blows and get me to bow and remove myself from that seat of authority, but my daddy is also a crown fixer and He'll easily come and adjust His daughter's crown when it's slipping. No matter what people call you, what they see you as or deem you to be, no matter how many attempts the enemy makes to strip this title and position from you. Sis, you are a Child of the King and He has chosen you to be called royalty. Sit like it, walk like it, talk like it, and most importantly, own it unapologetically. You are adopted into the greatest bloodline ever, one of royalty. God has given you the power and authority of a lifetime. That's why we must always know who we are and whose we are. The overall concept in my writing this book is to remind you of this. I pray today that as you read this, you'll find your seat of royalty. Fix that crown and remain.

Prayer: Father, thank you for choosing me to be an heir, for seeing me fit and deeming me worthy, even when I'm not everyone's first choice for the royal court. Thank you for selecting me to be a part of yours. God, help me to continue to see myself as you see me, to know that because of you I am graced for such positions of authority. Allow me to fix my crown and remain postured under you but above my enemies as you said in your word. Teach me to remain humble yet boast in you and who I am in you and because of you. Help me to confidently walk, talk, and act as if I am a part of a royal bloodline. As you fix my crown, help me to fix and adjust my sisters' crown that has been broken or tampered with. Show me how to be an etiquette coach in the spirit, showing them how to walk, talk, and act like royalty as well. Thank you for constant reminders of my belonging even when I doubt myself and the enemy wants to make me believe lies. Help me to live out every day of my life unapologetically as a Daughter of the King who was chosen and crowned in royalty. Amen.

Daughter

"Father of orphans and defender of widows is God in his holy habitation."–Psalms 68:5 CEB

In today's world "daddy issues" is a big topic and often times a pretty touchy subject for many who may not have experienced having a father growing up due to their father neglecting them, leaving, divorce, death, incarceration, separation or other circumstances which may have triggered and offset many other issues throughout the course of their lives. I often struggled with identifying myself as a Daughter of the King. I mean, seeing God as Abba and acknowledging my need and dependence on Him was almost impossible because I was one who had daddy issues I closed my heart off to receiving a father's love after dealing with years of what felt like disappointment and abandonment with my father being incarcerated throughout various periods of my life. Although my father is a great man and excellent provider I had to begin to be honest with myself and God and acknowledge that I was hurt and that there was pain there. I was beginning to allow the periodic absence of my father due to his incarceration to make me being to feel fatherless. This began to put a strain on our relationship it was damaging me inside I was becoming bitter, angry, and shut off to a father's love what I didn't see at first, but eventually got the revelation of was that it was too becoming a reflection of my relationship with my Heavenly Father. I was beginning to become distant, angry, easily disappointed, lacking trust, and feeling like I was on my own and didn't have that father figure to lean on. Little did I know that this would circle back around in my adulthood but this time it hit different this time God literally backed me into a corner where I had to begin to deal with everything that I was experiencing internally running from the pain was no longer an option. He wanted me to address these wounds and begin the healing process so that I could get back to loving Him and receiving Him as my father. The anger, bitterness, unforgiveness, and other deep rooted pain that I spent years masking had to finally be uprooted and healed. He came in and cleaned me up, all of the messy parts of my heart that had grown angry, bitter, and calloused towards my father, and He allowed me to receive His love as my father and through that, I was able to handle the unforgiveness and father wounds I had with my biological father. God even dusted the lens that I began to see him through and brought me to a place where I was able to accept him as my father again. I was able to learn to extend him grace and love on him because he, too, had a story and things that God needed to heal him of, and some of which I didn't know and understand that God would allow me to be a vessel for. This was truly the healing that I never saw coming that helped me in so many other areas of my life. God loves when we come to the place where we realize that we are too "I.N.D.E.P.E.N.D.E.N.T" or whatever the song says, and that we need Him and rely on Him as our Father. He enjoys the times where we let our hair down, take our hands off the wheel, and rest in Him, finally releasing our need for control and letting Him prove to us that He is our daddy and will always save the day. Today, I encourage you to rest in the Father's care and allow Him to love on you as His daughter. No matter what daddy issues you may have, or may have experienced one thing always remains that you are God's daughter and He loves you no matter what. There's literally nothing you can do to change His mind and nowhere that you can go to change that either.

Prayer: Father, I thank you for loving me and caring for me and all of my needs. Thank you for being the strength to my every weakness. Thank you for being who you are to me even when I don't deserve it, for loving me enough to never kick me out of your care and protection. Thank you for healing my heart in the areas where I have been hurt, rejected, and abandoned, that hold me back from receiving from you and even knowing how to come to you and others that you have strategically placed in my life during certain time periods for help. Continue to surround me with father figures and most importantly allowing me to take up my crown and rest in being your daughter. Forgive me for being prideful at times, disobeying you, ignoring you, or simply thinking that my plan and my way or my provision and ideas are better than yours operating out of fear that I am alone and have to do it all alone. I lay down my cares and concerns to you now. I ask that you will continue to let me see you, know you, and receive you as Father and provider of whatever I need whether it be love, peace, healing, provision, forgiveness, grace, mercy, a house, car, job or whatever I stand in need of. Let me be humble enough to come to you and make my request known. Teach me to trust you and lean on you when you are trying to stretch me and it becomes extremely uncomfortable. Let that be the times I lean in even more. Today, I relinquish control. I take the passenger seat and let you have the wheel. Continue to meet me at my point of need and allow me to become a vessel to others when you allow me to help them at their point of need. Most of all, remind me to trust your timing through it all and not become discouraged and jump ahead of you or fearful and stay behind you. Amen.

Daring Risk Taker

"Have I not commanded you? Be strong and courageous. Do not be frightened, and do not be dismayed, for the Lord your God is with you wherever you go."–Joshua 1:9 ESV

If you would've read this verse to me a few years ago, asking me to do some of the things God has been asking me to step out and do lately such as writing this book, launching a mentorship program, recklessly abandoning it all and moving to a new city, going back to school, quitting my job, starting a business, speaking, praying, and prophesying when He says, to just to name a few, honestly, I would've laughed in your face. In fact, apologizing about it now, I actually did this when God instructed me to do some things. I saw them halfway through or completely pulled a Jonah in some cases, as if I didn't even hear God, basically ignoring Him and laughing at Him. God is so funny and strategic though. I promise, everywhere that I went moving forward, someone was preaching on the story of Jonah or it would cross my timeline somehow and just like Jonah, God moved in my life the same. He brought everything full circle and allowed some instructions and opportunities to circle back around to me until I accepted the fact that I was called to take risks, leaps, and jumps of faith with God. Fear wasn't meant to control me and keep its grip on my life, suffocating me to remain uncomfortable in places God was calling me beyond, but I was too afraid and operating mediocrely, remaining in those things and places. I was allowing fear to be a master in my life. Fear will always present itself and we are called to be fearless, but there will be times where the fear honestly isn't going anywhere, but it will remain and try to make you afraid to take the daring risks that will launch you forward into destiny. So it'll literally pull up a chair and sit back and watch as you choose to stay where you are or do things even when fear has a front row seat in the audience, trying to intimidate you and talk you out of things. We are called to take the small steps God calls us to and be fearless, not because we are so brave, but because the more we learn to take the small steps in confronting fear, we literally take the next moves and fear less and less each time. Just as the story of Peter walking out on water in the Bible, God calls many of us to focus our attention on Him and listen for His directives. We're meant to be water walkers, we're meant to live a life requiring us to be a daring risk taker, even when we're presented with uncertainty and fear. For 24 years of my life, I was completely terrified of dogs. You wouldn't believe that girl that was once scared today now has two pit bulls whom she loves dearly. I would always compare my fear in my faith walk to that of my fear of dogs. At one point, I was completely afraid and terrified, to the point at times I was basically paralyzed when a dog came near, but I literally went in my room one day and cried out to God about this thing because it was holding me captive in ways I didn't like, such as missing out on family time because I was in my room afraid of the dogs. I figured the more afraid I became to answer God and do what He was telling me was the same. Being fearful and disobedient was only costing me on missing out on adventure with God and where He was leading me because I was stuck in fear. I reached a point where I realized if God could deliver me from a fear of dogs through a simple prayer—this is not to say I don't feel fear at all, but now I'm better able to acknowledge it, address it, and face it head on as the daring person that I am—it would the same case with anything else I feel the slightest fear with. I pray and then I allow God to give me the strength, courage, and boldness to dare take that task or assignment head on and face it, shaking and all. My days of being Jonah came to an end. I came to terms with embracing my inner Peter in his beginning stages of getting out of the boat. He was afraid but focused, courageous, bold, and defied all odds. One thing I learned with this faith walk is the small steps eventually add up and get you to where you want to go.

Prayer: Father, thank you for choosing me to be the one to take the risks that you call me to take. Take my hand and walk me through the journey. Wherever you will lead me, remind me that you are always with me whether it be near or far. When the enemy tries to impose paralyzing fear on me to keep me stuck, stagnant, and complacent, allow me to catch on to his schemes and break through them with your strength and anointing. Give me the grace to keep going when you say go, to keep doing when you say do, and the ability to discern when it's you versus when it's me, others, or the voice of the enemy trying to overpower you. Continue to keep me covered under your blood as I make bold, daring, risky moves that pave the way for others. Forgive me for the times you've called me to do something and I dropped the ball on the assignment out of fear and feeling inadequate or unequipped. Forgive me for the times where I was completely like Jonah and ignored you, doing what I knew to do and wanted to do. Thank you for loving me enough to allow me second chances to be obedient to your instructions, to follow your lead, and allowing you to stretch me beyond comfort. Thank you for giving me more courage and boldness to continue to face fearful situations and tasks head on even when fear is present. Allow your love to cover me and sit in my heart to cover every ounce of my fear. Let me keep taking small steps that equate to big moves. Let me be an example for others, that they'll learn to trust you and go and do more of what you're calling them to. Today I pray even the scary prayer that Jabez prayed: enlarge my territory, God, expand me and bless me indeed. Amen.

Evolving

"When I was a child, I spoke and thought and reasoned as a child. But when I grew up, I put away childish things." –1 Corinthians 13:11 NLT

I am like a photo hoarder and a journal hoarder, and something that I often love to do is take random moments to look through pictures and old journals to reflect on how far I've come since that particular season in life. Some seasons were tougher than others, but I survived each of them and I often find myself laughing and saying things like, "Oh what I would've went back and told Domonique from that year," "If only Domonique knew what she does now back then." I realized that although I say these things, it wasn't intended to happen that way. I had to go through what I went through in order to grow and learn the things I know now. There are things now that I know that I couldn't even have imagined knowing then, but because I'm an evolving human being who is growing with time, I do. Some seasons are often harder than others and you can't quite understand the pain you feel, but it's those necessary growing pains needed for that next level growth. The growing pains are necessary to squeeze out the wisdom of that season for another season. Your process of evolving is never completely about you, but often times God likes to use the wisdom you gained to teach others how to survive and evolve during their process. One thing about process and seasons of continuous growing pains and uncomfortability is that you grow better by the day if you allow it to happen. You should never reach a point where you've become all God has called you to be, until it's your time to take your final breath. There's more to learn, more to be done, more to experience, more levels to graduate, more risks to take, more improvements to make, and more wisdom and knowledge to be acquired. The woman writing this book now is not the same woman who initially got the book idea from God. In fact, after He gave me the idea, I experienced multiple seasons of growing pains and evolving to even write these words on this page now. The woman writing this book for you today won't even be the same in the next six months to a year from now, and I have no regrets about that as long as I grow better with time. Each year I find myself more, I become more solidified in my purpose, using my voice, and in my identity in Christ. I go through phases of decluttering and shedding, relinquishing myself from things, people, and places that no longer speak to my future or my growth. Each day I wake up and walk with Christ something changes, even if it's the most minor detail such as the way I think or speak. Each day I grow in healing and freedom, shedding dead weight, old mindsets, bad habits, old thought patterns and most importantly, the will to run from temptation, to run from the comfort zone and become the woman God wants me to be daily.

Prayer: Father, thank you for the growing pains that brought me to a new level in you. Thank you for using life's circumstances to stretch me, teach me, and grow me up. Thank you for never allowing anything to break me beyond that breaking point that you allowed. Thank you for constantly giving me strength to hang on even when the growing got tough. Help me to continue this process of evolving daily. Help me to relinquish to you old relationships, people, things, mindsets, behaviors, and patterns that no longer speak to my future self and who you're calling me to be. Lord, give me the focus to continue to grow and glow and be a woman who is daily evolving and inspiring other women to do the same. Let me look back days, weeks, months, and even years from now and see a different woman when I look in the mirror, one who is better but not done evolving. Teach me to remain humble and teachable, learning all that you want me to learn from each season of my life and from each experience I go through. Thank you for using everything I've experienced and gone through to shape me into the woman I am today, one who is truly ready to be used by you. Let me continue to be an inspiration and model for others. Let this day forward be the day that I vow to remain forward focused and no longer run to the comfort zones when the growing is uncomfortable. Increase even my faith, Lord. As I grow, take me to new levels in you. Amen.

Fearless

"For God hath not given us the spirit of fear; but of power, of love, and of a sound mind."–2 Timothy 1:7 KJV

Fear seems so small but screams so loud at many of us. Ironically, it often screams the loudest at the believers, the ones who often profess their faith in God and have to fight to let their beliefs, actions, and words align with their heart's sentiments. Well, at least I found this to be true for me. The same way that I spent years gripped by the fear of dogs, almost paralyzed and nonfunctional, I found that the little girl who was once bold and lived a life out loud developed a shell and outward layer of fear that attached itself to my life. Fear seemed to have had me bound. I was professing to be a believer, but my actions, thoughts, and affirmations weren't aligning. I found that the same way that I had to pray myself out of my fear of dogs and believe that God could do it was the same faith I had to have when it came to me standing up for my faith. There were opportunities that I passed on because I was afraid to do something, to say something, to be something in the room where it seemed that I didn't belong or that there were others superior to me. God delivered me of my paralyzing fear of dogs and began to shift my faith in believing Him for the same in my everyday life. If I must be honest, each day is a separate battle of its own. There are times where I have to wake up and show up, even when fear presents itself. I have to learn to speak up even when my voice is shaking. I have to be all God has called me to be even if I have trouble understanding it, believing it, or coming into agreement with it. I learned over time that fear will always try to peek its head, but it's my job to allow God to handle the outcomes and results of me doing things afraid and without restraint nor restriction. So even if I never become fully comfortable with something or even don't feel like doing it, as long as I set out and keep an open, available, and willing heart, I will conquer the bully called fear and remain fearless just as God created me to be. God didn't give us a spirit of fear but of power, love, and a sound mind. He reaffirms this in His word multiple times, that Love drives out fear and there's nothing that can separate us from His love, so where He is, fear can't even exist. We literally cast it out when we choose to be bigger than it, even though it screams that it is bigger. Resolve in your mind that you have a sound mind and even when you tremble, you are not too fearful or afraid to do what God has called you to do, to be all God has called you to be, or to show up and say what God wants you to say.

Prayer: Father, thank you for your love that covers all of my fears, worries, and anxieties. Show me how to show up in every room I enter and to every opportunity you present to me. Let me not run from it or remain trapped and bound by fear. Where Satan has tried to keep me gripped by fear and muzzled in silence, break it now. Teach me to acknowledge my feelings but not let them dictate how, when, and if I do what you want me to do. Teach me how to stare fear down and do it anyway. Remind me of the fact that you have called me to live boldly and live a life out loud. Remind me of how faithful you are and that you will always protect me, provide for me, and be present. Affirm me in times of weakness and remind me of who you have called me to be and of the power that you have given to me to overcome fear and anything the enemy throws my way. Let my faith scream loud and my actions, words, and thoughts align with your word and what you say and think about me. Amen.

Favored

"For the Lord God is a sun and shield; the Lord bestows favor and honor; no good thing does He withhold from those whose walk is blameless."–Psalms 84:11 NIV

There will be times where your resume with God speaks for itself. While, yes, there will be times that you are the top selection in some rooms, there will also be rooms that you enter where you're not so much in demand. In fact, they want to turn you down but God's favor just won't allow them to, or He allows it so that you go to where He is trying to strategically place you. That's just how favor operates. It puts you in places that you don't qualify for or even shuts doors on you that lead you to the correct door that God assigned to you with your name on it and with exactly what you need behind it. I've been in rooms and selected for things where I was the top pick for interviews, positions that I auditioned for, and other things. Then there was a time where God allowed doors to close on me and shift me. I'll share with you the time that I interviewed for a company, was selected and then let go before I could even begin the position. I was hurt, then a few years later God allowed me to see just how much He favored me by allowing me to be contacted by a place of employment that I never applied for, and I walked right into a job offer after a five-minute interview that felt more like an introduction to the company. In that very instant, I felt such peace and God reminding me of how He will favor me and put me where I belong without me having to force my way into places and spaces that He ordained for me. Sometimes God will allow you to experience those moments where out of everyone in the area, there's a different gracing and special thing for you. It's a little substance called God's favor, which makes people accept you when you don't understand why or how they ever could. It allows you to be the one selected out of the masses, it qualifies you for the things that you should and never could've imagined. It also allows you to do things that are seemingly impossible to others and allows you to receive that royalty treatment. Think it not strange if you enter into a season where things just seem to have your name all over it and people are preferring you and treating you a special type of way, as if you paid for valet parking, first class, or room service.

Prayer: Father, thank you for choosing me even when I don't choose myself or when others don't choose me. Thank you for allowing me to enter into a season where favor is literally about to chase me down. Allow my name to be in the rooms that I need to be in prior to my arrival. Father, thank you for reminding me that I am special in your sight and that there is a favor upon my life that will qualify me beyond what my resume says and what I can muster up in an elevator pitch. Remind me that although favor sometimes doesn't seem fair, let me not apologize for what you have allowed to happen to me and for me and receive it wholeheartedly. Thank you for loving me so much that you shower me with favor and allow me to stand out to others where needed and when needed. Forgive me for holding on to the sting of rejection. All of the times that I was turned away or told no, thank you for redirecting me and making me hold out for the right door, even when I didn't see it at the time. Thank you for loving me so much that you cancelled my plans and allowed yours to prevail. Show me favor as I move forward in all that I do. Allow there to be a gracing and anointing upon it and me that there will be a demand for whatever it is that I am doing at the time. Continue to get the glory out of my life and allow the naysayer to know that you have the final say and when you call me into season of repeated favor moves, nothing can stop the flow of that. Amen.

Forgiven

"You, Lord, are forgiving and good, abounding in love to all who call to you."–Psalms 86:5 NIV

I was doing an activity with a friend who encouraged me to take some time to sit and think about my full testimony and acknowledge what it is that I have to offer to the world through my story. In doing this activity, I came to realize that some things I avoided out of guilt, shame, unforgiveness towards myself and others, and I realized that what was holding me back from testifying should have been because God literally forgave me for it all and still forgives me daily. While this doesn't mean to exhaust that grace that God shows us daily, it does mean that I can truly come to Him with every messy part of me and talk to Him about it, because there's literally nothing that He doesn't know of and hasn't and won't forgive me of. Just like with Adam and Eve, the enemy often is the master of whispering lies. He likes to get into our ears and convince us that God doesn't love us and we've gone too far off track to even come to the point of return, or what we've done or experienced is just unforgivable and inexcusable. May I stop you right there in this very moment and debunk every lie that the enemy has fed you about God not forgiving you? It doesn't matter how far from God you have strayed; there's a place for you to return to with the Father. We all sin and no sin is bigger than another. God doesn't walk around with a scale comparing our sins nor does he keep a bag with our sins labeled and stored away for later, not at all. In fact, oftentimes we are the very ones who allow the devil to rehearse our sins with us in our heads and play out unrealistic scenarios about how God feels concerning us and those things. Again, let me debunk these lies. I'm on a mission to come for the enemy's throat this year, and that means me treading up in his camp and taking back God's beloved ones. So, sis, no matter where you are right now, I want you to stop and simply ask God to forgive you of (insert what you want Him to forgive you for) and thank God for his forgiveness in advance as you go your way. Also, know this, whatever you insert in the blank and choose to ask for forgiveness for, He already knows in advance, so you no longer have to be afraid of presenting these things to Him. It doesn't matter if you're struggling with unforgiveness, sexual impurity, lust, smoking, drinking, lying, cheating, addictions, whatever it is, bring it to Him. We have a forgiving Father, and in accepting that we are freed to be vulnerable with Him and others, as well as He walks us along the journey, the enemy is no longer able to keep us bound, stuck, trapped, muzzled, and in pain because of our painful pasts.

Prayer: Father, thank you for forgiving me time and time again, even when I chose to stay stuck in my mess. Thank you for coming into my heart and into my life, for seeing me fit enough to come in and clean me up, to forgive me and make me whole, to make me a testimony for others. Thank you for seeing beyond my flaws and seeing my needs, and one of those needs is consistent forgiveness. Thank you for loving me even in my mess, for reminding me that just as the prodigal son, I, too, can come home and you'll always be waiting there with your arms wide open, waiting to accept me and love me as if nothing happened. Thank you for forgiving me. I accept you as my Lord and Savior. Come into my heart, clean me up, and use me to testify of your saving grace, to testify of your redemptive power in my life. I believe in you and your work on the cross so that I can come to you and receive forgiveness, so that I may have life and not have to live in the darkness.

Allow me to continue to forgive those who hurt me, persecute me, try to harm me, slander me, and show me how to love on them so that they can experience your love and forgiveness too as I have experienced. Thank you for the freedom that I find in knowing that you've forgiven me and I no longer have to walk in guilt, shame, or condemnation, but in freedom. Amen.

Finisher

"So let's not get tired of doing what is good. At just the right time we will reap a harvest of blessing if we don't give up."–Galatians 6:9 NLT

Whenever I am on the verge of giving up and quitting, I remind myself it will get hard. It may seem tough, but I cannot throw in the towel. I, maybe like you too, am one who absolutely enjoys a good journal and some new pens. Every year I'd have a new journal, pens, and highlighters to track my goals, yet year after year I was seeing repeated patterns of unfinished products. I had to learn to extend myself some grace and learn to trust God's timing but on the other hand, I had to truly learn to take accountability for the unfinished business that God had already given me a go on. He'd give me the assignment or task and the provision and strategy, yet I'd still not complete it. I prayed and asked Him for guidance and to connect me with who I needed to connect with to get the help I needed. This is where my mentors and life coach came in my life and I began to see my goals from a different lens and go after them with a changed mindset, not feeling defeated or incapable. God began to remind me that we are all in a race of our own to the finish line and there's different things we'll have to do along the way. For some, it may be to go to school, start a business, write a book, launch that new line of merchandise, start that church or ministry. You'll be stretched and challenged along the way and if I could insert some type of screaming without screaming at you, I'll warn you that anything worth having won't come easy. You will become weary and experience some fatigue on the journey. What I've essentially learned on the way to the finish lines that God placed before me is that it's never about the finish line. As long as you get that it's so much bigger, it's about the process along the way, who you've become, but just know that the enemy is going to fight you hard on any of it, if it's anything that's going to strengthen your faith and help you bring God glory. I learned this on my way to receive my bachelor's degree. I experienced so many obstacles to even my acceptance that the six years it took me to graduate began to wear on me, especially when I lost my grandfather, who was my biggest supporter when it came to my education. I really wanted to throw in the towel, but God nudged me to get back in the fight, and May 2016 I walked the stage and received my degree. I have one even better, if you're a reaper of the fact that God pushed the finisher in me to complete this book, which was not by far easy, I experienced so much resistance and turmoil during this process. My biggest one was a battle with depression. I couldn't see the point in writing. Although I knew on the other side of this people would be healed, set free, and delivered, that prison doors would be unlocked for others, and that I had to finish, some days I struggled to see that finish line, but God. I want to encourage you today that no matter what you've started and seemingly quit on, that the finish line is still ahead waiting for you and it's time for you to get up and keep pressing toward, take those small steps daily that will land you right where you're trying to get to. Some days you may have to rest it out, others you'll have to fight it out in prayer, through praise, and other times you'll simply have to phone some back up for a little boost of encouragement and prayer that will thrust you forward and jumpstart you again.

Prayer: Father, thank you for the finisher's anointing that rests heavy upon my life. Allow this to be a season where it is reactivated. Give me a jumpstart and allow me to learn to pray, praise, and press my way through with you on my side and with the help of those that you have stocked my life with to help me jumpstart again and complete the tasks and assignments you have called me to. Thank you for bringing me back to your feet and helping me to find my strength in you when I grow tired, weak, and weary and it leaves me wanting to walk away and abort the missions. Father, lift my arms where they've grown weak, show me how to rest truly in you even in the midst of me working for you. Let me distinguish the rhythm and pattern to keep me on track to getting things done. Let me know when to stop and when to go. Let me not fall into a pit or cave due to fatigue, keep me refreshed, and push me to have a Thomas the Tank anointing and declaration on my tongue that I think and I know I can keep going regardless of what it looks like. Remove the need and want to procrastinate and let me take the things that you've called me to seriously and move in your divine timing. Keep the fire burning and the flames lit. Show me when I'm running low places to run for a refuel. Grace me to not only begin and do a thing but complete it in totality, as you are a finisher. Allow me to have that same gracing to start and finish a thing as you. Let me give it my all and do it diligently unto you. Bring everything I've been struggling to complete to a finish expeditiously. Amen.

Garden

"As for that in good soil, they are those who, hearing the word, hold it fast in an honest and good heart, and bear fruit with patience."–Luke 8:15 ESV

You reap what you sow (can't reap what you don't sow). I had this flower I was so excited to plant before, but like many of us, I grew impatient with it. I was tired of putting in work, checking it every single day, waiting to see the harvest yet seeing nothing. I grew weary and gave up on it. As I was sitting on my balcony, though, I happened to look down. Mind you, I haven't cared for it in forever, but apparently nature was still doing its thing and boom, it sprouted. At that moment, the Holy Spirit spoke to me about how we are just as gardens, and those little flower pots that God puts a few seeds in and waters, nurtures, loves, and provides for will soon return an investment on what was sown. God expects a return on the seeds (time, talent, money, treasure that He gives us) because He didn't plant things in us for no reason or to allow them to sit and die, but because He saw us as good soil to plant in to receive the return from, to see growth, to see something bloom from what was planted. For some of us, maybe it's time to use those things God has placed down in us or gifted us with to scatter some seeds. Don't wait for the perfect conditions. Today is the day to get to work and allow those seeds to take root so that they can be watered and grow roots that will produce something to produce more seeds in those around us. Understand that if God invested something in you, He saw you as good ground to plant in so He can expect His return. You are like the garden that never dies but constantly reproduces, even in the dry seasons. Sometimes that one sprout is all God expects, as long as we don't disconnect from Him, the source of our growth and existence. It's time to tend to the things God has entrusted us with and allow those things to grow and multiply. For others, maybe it's time to go back and tend to the thing God planted that you may have uprooted too fast, refusing to be planted and blooming there. There's seed time and then there's harvest. Another important thing for seeing the cultivation of something you planted is creating an atmosphere conducive for growth. Check yourself and ask, is your soil tainted? Is it going to waste? Or is it simply not conducive for the returned harvest that God wants on His investment? And if so, what can you do to fix that? Water it, give it some TLC, feed it the Word. It's Harvest Time!! It's time to plant, cultivate, and watch it grow.

Prayer: Father, thank you for seeing me as good garden soil to plant seeds into that you will help me to cultivate and cause to grow so that you can receive a return on your investment. Forgive me for allowing my soil to become dry at times and kill off what you began in me. Show me to water myself with the Word and allow what you've placed down in me to take root and bloom, so the growth will be evident and visible. Father, thank you for allowing me to stay connected to you and never try to grow things without you and out of season. Show me to move as you move to allow the new seeds to scatter where needed so they, too, can grow. Lord, I pray that I will flow with you and know when it's seedtime and when it's harvest time. Allow me to not grow impatient in the process but to remain planted so things can take root and grow in me and through me. Let my soil not be tainted and damaging for what you want to produce through my life, but let it be good ground for cultivation and growth. Let this be the season where I produce effortlessly and continue to get the glory from it all. Keep me healthy and spiritually nourished, loved, and cared for. Amen.

Giant Slayer

"And David inquired of the Lord. saying, 'Shall I pursue after this troop? Shall I overtake them?' And He answered him, 'Pursue, for thou shalt surely overtake them and without fail recover all.'"–1 Samuel 30:8 KJV

Reading this verse, I always get chills because it takes me to reflecting on the story of David and Goliath and how he quickly learned that size didn't matter but his obedience, his courage, and his availability was what helped him overcome and defeat Goliath. David was stronger than he thought. Oftentimes, we underestimate the power that lies within us to overcome the giants we face throughout life. These Goliaths manifest themselves in the form of fear, anxiety, doubt, depression, sickness, diseases, poverty, brokenness, people, and whatever else the enemy can throw at us. One thing we must realize is that it's important to always know and acknowledge our weaknesses and speak to that very thing, because those are the areas the enemy attacks the most, but just like David, you may currently be facing some Goliaths that seem big in size but like David, have to come and realize that you just may very well be the one called upon to take it down. This Goliath may have been running rampant in your family for a while or in your life for a while, and you've probably experienced some weakness, some weariness, and felt yourself waver in your strength, almost succumbing to a place of defeat. But I urge you to understand that nothing the enemy throws your way is too impossible for you to overcome. God tells us in His word that with Him all things are possible. He equipped us with armor for the battle, the belt of truth, breastplate of righteousness, helmet of salvation, sword of the spirit, shield of faith, and gospel of peace. Goliath had five rocks for his slingshot and you have six tools. You're even more equipped than him, and he won the battle with one shot. What are you waiting for? Each day, take on your armor and give the enemy a run for his money. We don't fight against flesh and blood, so no need to waste that type of energy. Literally, sister, pick up your armor and fight. If you've thrown in the towel, it's time to tap into your inner power and authority Christ has given you and get back in the fight. Just as David asked shall he pursue, if you are reading this today, God is giving you the go to get in the fight and pursue after your enemy, recover everything he has stolen from you, and take over his kingdom. You are THEE GIANT SLAYER and that's that, nothing more nothing less. You're enough, so every time a Goliath raises its head, OFF WITH IT! Size doesn't matter, it's you God wants to use, so give him that yes today, conqueror.

Prayer: Father, thank you for helping me to see the conqueror within me, the one who was chosen to pursue, recover, and overtake all that my enemies present to me. No matter what, help me to overcome whatever Goliath presents itself, whether it be physical, spiritual, mental, or emotional attacks. Remind me that through you I can do all things including overcome anything that comes my way. Teach me to not depend or lean on my own strength and understanding but to allow you to be my strength, shield, and protector. Give me boldness, confidence, and courage as I give you my "Yes" to face things head on with you by my side. Help me to not throw in the towel or allow defeat, weariness, or discouragement to become or remain my story. Thank you for even showing me what is behind each attack in the spirit realm and giving me practical and spiritual ways to deal with it. Let me no longer feel enslaved to fear or challenged by my size or the amount of power or authority that I have. Open my eyes to the way you've equipped and chosen me. Cover my fears with your love and allow me to slay every Goliath in my presence. Let the narrative be off with their head. Sharpen my sling and stones, teach me to properly wear my armor and use it to my full advantage. Amen.

Glass Shatterer

"For I can do everything through Christ, who gives me strength."
Philippians 4:13 NLT

Witnessing the United States of America swear in its first female vice president was an indicator to something within me spiritually. It symbolized that there are oftentimes where there is no blueprint in front of you and you'll be called to be the one to break the glass ceilings and boxes that have been put in place to keep you from achieving certain goals or from crossing certain barriers. Especially when patterns, cycles, and systems have been the same for so many years prior to it and you come along trying to break free and switch up the flow, doing something different, introducing something new to the old things. There's times where you are called to be the curse breaker in your family, where your bloodline has been stuck in poverty, dysfunction, lack, brokenness, and others things that have kept you in the cycles as well. But you've gotten into the secret place with God and mustered up the strength to tell hell to loosen its grip and set you free, because you have some new things to introduce to your bloodline. There's times where you'll be called to put on one heel and place it on the devil's neck, while on the other foot lacing up your bootstrap and going to war for what's rightfully yours and demand your bloodline be free from bondage. If you spend some time reflecting on some of the patterns and cycles you've noticed in your family, you'll find the very thing you're called to bring about a change to is the very thing that the heel you put on your foot, will come to shatter. Sometimes, trying to break free and do something new or set out to accomplish some things and be successful, will call for multiple attempts. Don't allow failure the first go-round cause you to quit and believe that it will never come to pass or be conquered. You have power within you to annihilate everything you set out to do, all of those God-given dreams, goals, and assignments. For many of you reading this right now, it's truly time for you to accept that you are the one that God is calling to break those generational curses that have existed for your family for so long. Don't despise the small steps you're taking and small choices and sacrifices you are making, nor the multiple tries that you've had to make. They are never failures, they are stepping stones that are leading to the breakthrough. Remember the Word tells you that God is within you, you cannot fail, and that's that. Not only is quitting not an option, but failure isn't. It's simply a push to stay in the game and keep going, thriving, soaring, and winning.

Prayer: Father, thank you for choosing me to be the one to acknowledge the cycles and patterns that have been upon my life and on my bloodline for years. Thank you for giving me the wisdom, strategy, and insight on how to navigate through and shatter the glass ceilings and break free from the generational curses that have tried to hold me back, hold my bloodline back, and even hold my sisters back. Thank you for letting me not grow weary or frustrated that it may take a while sometimes or that it may be a little harder than expected at times. Let me break free as you strengthen me to do so. Remind me that no matter how many times I fall, that I will never fail with you by my side. Continue to help me to use every stepping stone to get to the goal. Let me accomplish every God-given dream, gift, and goal and never let quitting be an option because with you, I can't fail. Father, let the breaker's anointing rest upon my life even now and come against everything that is trying to suffocate me and trap me into the patterns and cycles. Let freedom be my portion, show me what I am called to break. Let the curse-breaker anointing hit me even now and nothing ever remain the same. Remind me when I think I'm not enough that I was chosen for the task and I am qualified to do whatever you've called me to including breaking curses off of my bloodline. Let me lace up my boots and continue to go to war for what's mine and everything attached to me and at the same time, let me put on my heel and break through the box that tries to trap me in. Amen.

Glow Stick

"You are the light of the world. Like a city on a hilltop that cannot be hidden."–Matthew 5:14 NLT

Growing up, I enjoyed roller blading and going to the skating rink on Wednesday nights with my family for gospel skate night, but one of my favorite parts of the night was when they would cut off all of the lights and allow everyone to take out their glow sticks and let them light up the room while the music played and the room went wild. The Christian walk is kind of similar. The darkness is surrounding us daily and God is calling for us, His children, to be the glow sticks to light up the room. He requires us to shine a light on them. As we shine our lights, others' lights are illuminated and their world is lit up. They come to experience life and the light. Sometimes trying to be the light in the darkness can be a great task with so much darkness going on in the world, but it's never impossible to just show up and be. There's beauty in shining your light. Another thing I've come to the realization of is that being the light and walking through the Christian walk won't always be a walk in the park, but just as those skating rink nights, it has its fun side. God didn't call any of us to be boring, dull, or hide out in the background. It actually does God and others a disservice when you hide what's in you. So step up, show up, and shine. It's the time where your light is needed the most. Sometimes God will have to break you and shake you like that glowstick to get that light to shine, but you will shine and be a light in someone's world.

Prayer: Father, thank you for the light that you've placed down inside of me. God, even when you have to shake me up and break me, allow me to know that it's for my good and your glory and let my light shine. Father, just as you came in and lit up my world, allow me to go out into the world and be the light in someone else's world. Let me not miss an opportunity to shed some light and spread some love where it is needed most. Shine on the dark areas of my life so that I may keep letting my life and light illuminate every room I walk into. Let the warmth from my life melt away someone else's pain and lead them to you. When darkness tries to overpower my light, Father, let me not dim my light nor feel the need to hide it. Let me not despise the times where I may have to go alone and be the only light in the room, but cause me to use that as a reason to glow harder and shine even more. Help me to keep a fresh yes for you to be the light. Remind me of how fun this walk can be even in the hard times. Amen.

Healed

"But he was pierced for our transgressions, he was crushed for our iniquities the punishment that brought us peace was upon Him and by His wounds we are healed."–Isaiah 53:5 NIV

Many things in life can come to hurt us. They leave us bruised, scarred, and oftentimes leave our hearts bleeding. Someone rejects you? Now you've got a scar. Someone abandons you? There's another scar. A friend betrays you? Now you're bruised and afraid to trust. Your lover breaks your heart, now you are scared and never want to love again. For many, this leads to them bleeding out onto others, while for others it causes them to run from the pain and feelings of discomfort the broken and unhealed areas of life have brought them, and into the hands of the Father. When I think of healing, I picture the woman with the issue of blood who suffered for 12 years, literally dragging herself to Jesus. This is a visual of what many of us look like trying to get healed, crying out to God to relieve us from the pain whether it be physical, mental, spiritual, or emotional, because we're tired, weary, and frustrated from the years of pain we've had to endure. We just want to get to Jesus. Jesus reminds us in the text that by His stripes we are healed. Everything we would ever need healing from, He already paid a price for us on the cross and healing is available. God takes many of us on a journey of healing and we don't even realize that the healing was and never will be about us. It's for our good but for God's glory. When we heal, we are able to become a healing balm in the earth for others to have a safe space to heal. We are able to serve as the bridge for others to get to Jesus to receive their healing. Think about the story of the four friends who carried their sick friend on the mat through the roof to get to Jesus. This is a visual image of what we are called to be for many, a bridge to carry others over. We help bear their burdens, we learn how to get into the trenches with them and pull them up to where they need to be but can't get to alone. But this must first come through us having our own personal encounter with God and being healed ourselves. Just as hurt people bleed on others, healed people do too. The healing balm explodes and others begin to experience healing in various areas of their lives. In this life we've been equipped with various tools for healing, both spiritual and practical. Serving in this counseling role for the past year has definitely taught me that those with bleeding hearts easily bleed on others, but there are tools available to heal whether it's in prayer, deliverance, counseling, or through community. Community was one in which God used for me personally, but the healing process led to the beautiful discovery that a healed heart can literally heal a heart. One last disclaimer when it comes to healing: you may find yourself going in circles fighting for your freedom and deliverance. You'll naturally want to cope and revert to what has been medicine to those wounds (drinking, smoking, sex, partying, money, etc.), and this phase is never pretty, but you have to remember to never give up on your healing journey. Experience it all and allow God to guide you through. Remind yourself that this is just that, a phase, and on this journey as you evolve, you are going anywhere but back.

Prayer: Father, thank you for bringing awareness to the broken areas in my life that need to be addressed. Thank you for not only shining a light on them to show me what needs work but also for equipping me with the resources and tools to get healing, whether it be through digging in your word and my devotion time with you, signing up for counseling, or even being surrounded by those with language for what I've experienced and the way I can get through. Let me not become ashamed and afraid to address the broken and unhealed areas but rather run towards you as I lean into your healing virtue. Thank you for sending me those who will literally love me back to health and a place of healing. God, I come to you today as the woman with the issue of blood, crawling and all, simply with the willingness to be healed. Show me what to do to experience your healing. Help me to no longer go backwards and revert to old habits and coping mechanisms or stay in a place of stuck. Although healing may sometimes feel uncomfortable and inconvenient, help me to know that you can take me as I am and restore me. Make me whole again, touch my mind, body, and soul so that I'll no longer bleed on others but be that healed heart that releases healing balms to heal hearts. Thank you for covering me and every broken part of me. Thank you for surrounding me with people to keep me covered in love as I heal. God, I love you and thank you for being my great physician, for taking all of my pain, bruises, scars, and brokenness with you to the cross so that I may experience your divine and total healing. Amen.

Heavy Weight

"And we all, who with unveiled faces contemplate the Lord's glory, are being transformed into his image with ever-increasing glory, which comes from the Lord, who is the Spirit."–2 Corinthians 3:18 NIV

The enemy has a way of making us seem small, but if you like science, like myself, and learned about the term matter, matter is anything that takes up space. You are a representation of matter and you literally matter. You have a purpose, you have a voice, and you have a space that is specifically occupied for you. Sometimes there are rooms that you will step into that literally were awaiting your arrival. The room may have been missing something until you stepped in. There have been places where I've entered and noticed that a spirit of darkness seemed to hover over the atmosphere. Through prayer, God often revealed to me what to pray for and over as well as what was taking place. He also revealed that regardless of how much it seemed that darkness was hovering over the place in the spirit, I was bigger than any agenda of the enemy. Times I thought I was small, useless, muted, and backed away, God was showing me that I was a true heavy weight in the spirit and that I carried His glory with me everywhere that I went. Through the power of the Holy Spirit, I had the power within me to shake up rooms and atmospheres by commanding the room and decreeing and declaring things in prayer. When God's spirit resides in me when I carry the weight of God's glory, all darkness must bow and flee. This is to encourage those who the enemy has tried and tried for so long to back into the corner, to let you know that you are in the ring but don't have to be backed into a corner or made to be small any longer, because you are the heavyweight champ carrying God's glory with you everywhere you go. Remember that you matter, heavyweight, you are the walking representation of Christ in the earth and as you enter a room, people encounter God. They become engulfed in being in your presence because you carry God's presence with you. Where you are present, there is room and an opportunity for the Holy Spirit to show up and show out to manifest Himself like never before.

Prayer: Father, thank you for helping me to continue to prioritize you and get into your presence, so the more time I spend with you I can become more and more like you. Father, teach me to walk into rooms and allow you to shift, shake, and even transform the atmosphere. Engulf me with your presence everywhere I go and allow others to have an encounter with you when they are in my presence. Allow me to continue to make room for the Holy Spirit in my everyday life and be a manifestation of you in the earth wherever I am. When I am in rooms and situations that haven't seemed to change, teach me to flow with the Holy Spirit's work and notice even the smallest changes He is making. Show me how to discern when your presence is upon me and how to embrace it. Teach me to no longer draw back from the enemy but to grow with you and in confidence of who I am and the heavyweight that I am in the spirit. Continue to let me be a conduit carrying your love, peace, joy, light, salvation, and message throughout the earth. When they see me, let them see you. Remove me out of the way. God, remind me that when I step into the room, that because you live in me, you entered the room with me, and I don't have to retreat because all darkness must flee. Amen.

Helping Hand

"He made himself nothing, by taking on the very nature of a servant."– Philippians 2:7 NIV

Oftentimes, we can complicate the plan of God when it comes to finding our purpose. We make these to-do lists and lists of goals and accomplishments that we want to reach, so much so that we can tend to get lost in titles, positions, deadlines, and places, forgetting to exist in the moment. And aside from making our plans, we forget to allow room for God to alter those plans. As I'll soon be exiting my 20s, I reflect now and realize how many nights I spent crying myself to sleep because I was searching for God's plan for my life and what my purpose was. Sometimes, I'd even write letters to Him with tears streaming down my face, asking Him why was I even here and if I was needed. While I was busy crying out to God and doing all of the talking, I wasn't allowing myself to take time to listen and look at what He was showing me. That I was walking in my purpose all along: whether I was at McDonald's working the drive-thru, in the classroom teaching my students, or even in the community working with clients. The puzzle pieces didn't connect until later down the line, that all along, regardless of where I was, there was always an assignment attached to me being there, and that was to be the helping hand. I learned that I was the hands and feet of Jesus and there'd be times I go to work to teach but find myself praying during my lunch break. I'd go into the community to assist a client and I was being a listening ear because they were a few minutes from committing suicide. You don't have to overthink the plan of God if you constantly keep at the forefront of your mind that no matter what position you hold or where you are, that you are and will always be a servant and be the hands and feet of Jesus in the earth, no matter the room you are in. If you remain humble and allow Him to work, He will take you from working drive-thrus to mounting platforms, but understand that the main objective never changes. You are where you are to serve and if you do so diligently unto Him, He will elevate you in due time but also, you will have peace and find happiness when you are content. You are and always will be essential and have purpose. Someone somewhere needs you and the help you have to offer.

Prayer: Father, thank you for helping me to always see myself as your servant. No matter where I am, let me do everything that I am doing diligently unto you. Father, let there be less of me and more of you. Allow me to take the goals, dreams, and visions that I have and do them unto you, but remind me to allow you to direct my steps and path on where you want me to be and what capacity you want me to serve in. Teach me to never serve out of obligation, greed, or any other wrong motives, but let me operate in serving with a spirit of love. Show me that the sacrifices that I have to make in some seasons lead to even greater in other seasons, and remind me that they don't go in vain. Transform my heart, search me o God, let my heart be right in all that I do. Give me the strength I need to continue to persevere daily. Let me know and rest in your promise that I will never miss anything promised to me or any opportunity. Thank you for the privilege to be chosen to be your servant. Continue to reveal yourself to me and the plans that you have. Keep me aligned with where I should be in each season. When I get overwhelmed by thinking I am behind in your plan or that I've missed the mark, allow me to debunk the lies of the enemy and remind me to breathe and rest in your promise to lead me and guide me. Use me, Lord, however you please. Let me stay open to your guidance, direction, and correction. Let new doors locate me in this season as I continue to say yes to you and serve in the capacity that you will have me serve. Let me begin to see how that seemingly pointless phase of my life was serving as a catapult for where you are taking me. Let me never lose my footing and always stay humble and grounded in you, even as I experience increased elevation. Amen.

Hot Girl

"He sends His servants like flames of fire."–Hebrews 1:7 NLT

As I was beginning this writing session, I decided to light some candles, as they help me to get into the zone and allow me to ease my mind from all distractions. As I was lighting this one candle, though, Holy Spirit began to minister to me about the fire that was lit. I could almost envision a room full of lit candles. You know how oftentimes, for a birthday party we take one candle and light all of the other candles on the cake? Well, might I suggest that this walk with Christ has shown itself to be a similar representation. I began to reflect on the start of Christ beginning a work in me and how it seemed so pointless and mundane and some days, painful. Life's experiences seemed to be lighting me up alright, but I thought I was the one being set ablaze. In actuality, I was, but one thing He promised is I wouldn't be consumed no matter what was thrown my way, and I'd never leave the battle smelling like smoke, only setting other things ablaze. The tougher life's experiences became and tests and trials presented themselves, it was as if fuel was being added to the fire. I wanted this fire to be contained and to cease, but God had a plan. He was allowing all that I was going through to set me on fire so much that I began to speak up and tell the world my story. I began to share my testimony, my experiences and the wisdom and insight that I had gained through all of those wilderness experiences, and as I began to share, here's where the representation of the fire plays a part. Over time, the fire that was lit within me was beginning to spread to others that became affected by the words that Holy Spirit gave me to speak. They became encouraged, more knowledgeable on God's goodness and who He was. Then, guess what? They, too, began to take that fire started within them and go light fires in others. In our society, it's often looked down upon to be a Firestarter, or arsonist as we would call it, but in the kingdom, that's what it's all about. Taking your fire and beginning to impact others in your reach and out of your reach. God used fire to develop me, prune me, and allow only the things that were necessary to my current season to remain, because if it had no significance and couldn't withstand God's fire in my life, it was consumed. Some of the things that were consumed included relationships, jobs, old mindsets and habits, possessions, things that were hardening my heart, and anything else that couldn't survive the next level with me. That is when I noticed a shift in my life and the impact that was being made on others. During that time, especially in the beginning of that season, I would've wished for it to end or not even come but if you ask me today, I would truly not change a thing because I wouldn't be the woman I am today without that season, without that experience in the wilderness, without the wildfire being set ablaze in me to help set ablaze in others. I made a vow to God to allow Him to use the fire in me to consume and set everyone in my path ablaze until all have experienced the lit life in Christ.

Prayer: Father, thank you for the seasonal winds that have blown my way and caused the flames to move and shift areas of my life. Thank you for helping me to learn to trust you in the difficult seasons and remind me that you are in control and working it all for my good. Thank you for allowing me to know that one thing stands, that no matter what fires I undergo, I'll never smell like the smoke and flames that tried to consume me and the fire within me. Father, the fire that burns down within me shows me how to use it for the good to set ablaze everything and everyone in my path with the power and anointing that lies within me. Remind me that sometimes I'll have to start small but that the fire will end up being like a wild forest fire, because I give you my Yes and my vow to take everyone with me and let them experience a taste of that fire burning within them so that they, too, may walk in purpose and turn up the flames for the Kingdom as well. Every time I forget how lit I am, you remind me and allow me to come back to that realization. Use every ounce of the fire within me for you glory, God, until all have heard and experienced you. May my assignment forever be to fuel flames and ignite fires. Amen.

Influencer

"Iron sharpens iron, so people can improve each other."–Proverbs 27: 17 NCV

Have you ever caught yourself conforming to your friend group? Workplace? Or environment? Or seeing others amongst you do the same? In a world where social media is a major part of influence and so many are striving to be on a platform and have a blue verified checkmark by their name to make them feel special and important, we must not lose sight of how important we are right where we are. God may call you to many platforms and even to the nations, but the way to those things starts right where we are in the home, workplace, community, relationships, and friendships. Even our encounters with strangers remind us of the influence that we have. You may impact a person's life through one encounter that changes them that then goes and changes others. Even if millions aren't following you and sharing your posts or giving you shout-outs on a regular, right where you are, you are making a difference. You are helping change someone's mindset, behavior, attitude, posture, and even their skillset. The impact that you are making today may ring through the nations through one encounter, so never feel that because you don't have a blue checkmark, millions of followers, or aren't being called on to speak at an event that you don't have influence, because you do, and it starts right where you are. Someone needs you, and that is why you are exactly where God has you positioned in this season. I've been surrounded by others who have challenged some of my behaviors, ways of thinking, and more that have helped shaped me into the woman that I am today, and I am now witnessing myself having the opportunity of sharing some of the things that I've learned and what God imparts in me to take it and use it in my spheres of influence. And I'll keep going until all have heard, seen, and learned, even if I never mount a platform or have a blue check by my name. Friends, family, coworkers, strangers, and others will continue to be impacted and changed by my presence in their life and me carrying God's glory. Remember that you have power within you to affect others through your interactions and engagement.

Prayer: Father, thank you for the spheres of influence you have given me and let me not take for granted the opportunities that you present to me to be used for your glory right where I am. Remind me when I forget that I am qualified to be in the rooms that I am. Thank you for teaching me to use my voice and not be silenced because I think that I have nothing to say. Let me be your voice and speak what you tell me to. Through my actions, speech, and life, may others' lives be changed at home, in the workplace, in my relationships and friendships, even amongst the strangers that I encounter, let me make a difference. Father, let me make a difference in one life that will even go and change others' lives. Remind me that platforms and blue checks don't define me and who I am or the difference that I make. Even if the people never scream my name, may they come to know you more through me, let my light continue to shine, and even when it seems dull, reignite it. God, let my character always have the capacity to handle the spaces that I am in and let me not get into places my character is not ready to handle. As you continue to develop me, let me use what you teach me to teach others. Let me even have an indirect influence on the lives of others. Let me continue to shake up systems that aren't aligned with you and your will for your glory. Amen.

Intended

"For if you keep silent at this time, relief and deliverance will rise for the Jews from another place, but you and your father's house will perish. And who knows whether you have not come to the kingdom for such a time as this."– Esther 4:14 NIV

As I wrote this, I could almost imagine the sound of screeching tires skidding across the road stopping you in your tracks. Oftentimes, the enemy will use our own insecurities, doubts, and thoughts to attack us, our circumstances, or even those around us. He will have us believing that we are an accident or that we don't belong, or the biggest thing that I took away from this verse, that we have nothing to offer, when according to this text it tells us the complete opposite. You were indeed calculated in God's timing to be on the earth the exact day that you were born. So for me, August 30, 1992 was an important day, and the next important day was when I decided to begin this book because I know that it speaks to my purpose and God allowed me to see that there was something that needed to be said from me directly from Him. There was something that I had to give to the world. All of these years I was holding a necessary answer to someone's dilemma. Surprisingly, the enemy had me believing otherwise. All along, I was hiding out in a cave, I was muzzled, I was insecure and lacking in my ability to see myself as God saw me or even act like it. I almost believed that my parents conceived me on an accident and that my birth was pointless but as of today, I say not so. I pray that as you have read this page and go back to read the scripture in Esther, that you, too, will see that like myself and like Esther, you were called, chosen, equipped, and quite frankly, you are the one that God chose to be where you are, doing what you're doing. Don't run from it and most importantly, don't be afraid of it and feel bad for where you are, because it's where God has placed and you don't have to apologize. You are not a mistake, you were intended. God placed you in the equation and factored in your existence. Never consider yourself or your life a mistake, even if someone speaks that over you. Just as Esther, David, Noah, Abraham, and many others, you are the one God selected and intended to be here and doing that very task. So, settle into that place and get moving for the kingdom.

Prayer: Father, thank you for choosing me and reminding me that I am not an accident, mistake, or problem, but I was intended. Meaning you strategically calculated and factored me into your plan for such a time as this. Thank you for choosing me time and time again, even when I run or have trouble seeing this for myself. Thank you for helping me to get this resolve in my heart that I, (Insert Your Name) was born for such a time as this. Thank you for surrounding me with those who will speak life into me and affirm me. Remove all the negative naysayers from around me and those that I can't control. Thank you for helping me to silence and drown out the death that they try to speak into my existence. Help me to pick up the mantle that you have placed upon me and allow me to carry out every assignment to completion. Thank you for making me a miracle and for letting me be the answer for someone, reminding me that someone is waiting on me and my yes, as I am literally the miracle and answer to their dilemma. Remind me, Father, that you are the giver of life and gave me life, and you entrust me to give life to others. Let me not take that for granted nor despise that you've placed me here or gave me the opportunity to bear life and give someone else a chance to live out their God-given purpose. Help me to never abort any of my God-given assignments, tasks, and missions. Amen.

Jesus Girl

"I have been crucified with Christ. It is no longer I who live, but Christ who lives in me. And the life I now live in the flesh I live by faith in the Son of God, who loved me and gave Himself for me."–Galatians 2:20 NIV

This verse just makes me think of so many different things. One, that God loves me so much and calls me His own. He thought enough to allow His only son to take my place. I'm truly loved and truly His girl, but thankfully, with Him, the honeymoon phase never ends. I'll forever and always be His girl. Second, when I received Jesus, His blood washed me clean and made me brand new. I'm practically a dead woman walking, but it's Christ living in and through me vicariously being exuded in the earth now because of one simple yes. I lived in church throughout my childhood: weekly services, practices, prayer breakfasts, conferences, lock-ins you name it I was there. It became one of the main things that I was known for, being the "church girl." I often despised being associated with this because it made me seem like some sort of outcast. I'd find even the smallest ways to blend in, but no matter what. the light in me always outshined any act I was putting on for people. People would ask me the strangest questions. all reverting back to the main question. "You're a church girl. aren't you?" Over time, I realized that it wasn't so much that I despised being called this, but it had more to do with the fact that I was called to so much more than just the four walls of a church building. The fire, passion, and burning desires within me knew that there was more. God was calling me to spread the gospel in many other arenas. The workplace, marketplace, social media, grocery stores, gas stations, hospitals, nursing homes, and wherever I went. Regardless of if people referred to me as "church girl," I began to understand that it was bigger than that and bigger than me. Something clicked in me and I realized that it was time for the Jesus in me to be taken everywhere I went and be allowed to shine through. A shift began to take place in my walk with Christ, I began experiencing closeness and true relationship with Him. Christ. A light switch came on. I literally began to spend so much time with Christ even outside of church that I developed that Jesus girl glow, one that I couldn't hide. It's something special when you make a decision to no longer walk in religion and believe simply because it was instilled in you by others but now you have revelation and believe firsthand because of your own personal encounters and experiences.

Prayer: Father, thank you for opening my eyes and bringing me out of the mindset of religion that once tried to entangle me, causing me to try to master this walk perfectly, crossing every T and dotting every I, all while missing the importance of simply walking step by step and day by day in relationship with you. Thank you for shifting me to a new place in you, for helping me to grow, to know you better, and walk with you, allowing myself to be loved and love on you. Thank you for letting my walk with you impact others, for giving me that undeniable Jesus glow that becomes contagious to everyone I come in contact with so much that they can't deny your existence or our relationship. Let it lead them to you. Thank you for letting me die to flesh and lay down my life daily so that you can vicariously live through me and be honored and carried out into the earth. Thank you for letting me be a willing and available vessel. Continue to allow my light to shine and keep a glow upon my face as you grow to show me new aspects of you.

Let me grow to embrace that I may have once been called a church girl, or on the opposite end, may have never even stepped foot in a church, but because you live in me I will always be known as a Jesus girl. Thank you for the reminder that this walk isn't about me but it's actually beyond me and meant to be taken into any sector of the earth you send me in, whether it be right in my home or in another part of the world. Amen.

Kingdom Focused

"But seek first the kingdom of God and His righteousness and all these things shall be added unto you."–Matthew 6:33 KJV

A countdown from 10 to 1 and "Ready or not here I come" from everyone but the seeker followed by a quiet silence filled the room, because the others in the room were busy focused on something else or running and hiding to not be found. Sounds familiar? Something that we do with God sometimes, is we're either off occupied with our own agendas and plans while God wants some one-on-one time with us, or we're busy trying our hardest to run and hide from Him because He's calling us deeper and we feel a little uncomfortable the further out we go. I observed a group of children playing hide-and-go-seek and watched as the person who was "it" to go do the seeking was filled with excitement, ready to discover all of their opponents as they diligently sought after them. This reminded me of how I want to be and am called to be with God in a position of seeking Him and minding Kingdom business, letting Him allow me to be carefree from the stresses and concerns of life that try so hard to pre-occupy me and my time, pulling me from the Father. God wants us to be diligent in our pursuit of Him because the deeper we go, the more we walk closely with Him. He invites us into new levels of intimacy with Him, reveals more secrets to us, and allows us VIP access to Him. We no longer walk on the outer courts with Him, but we are the homies in the inner court and sometimes even behind the veil that depends on our individual seek. Inside of each of us is a space that only God can fill. He allows this to draw us deeper into Him and keep us Kingdom focused so no matter how much we chase houses, cars, degrees, promotions, titles, sales, clout, or other material possessions, it will never be enough to fill us up. We are meant to be focused on the Kingdom, allowing God to take care of the rest of the things we want. When we seek Him, He takes care of all of our other needs and even throws in some of the things that we want.

Prayer: Father, thank you for the access you have given me to you to be able to walk in communion and relationship with you in such close proximity. Forgive me for the times when I was pre-occupied or distracted by things and not focused on the Kingdom agenda and assignments before me. Show me how to become more grounded in you and spend more time in your presence even when life becomes demanding. Teach me to prioritize and schedule with you being number one. Let me never chase anything else to fill my void when I have complete and total access to you. Show me how to press beyond the veil, reveal to me secrets unknown, and let me be best friends with you. When I run away like Jonah, redirect me right back to you just as you did him. Thank you for always receiving me back with open arms. Remove the idols out of my way and let me let you take your rightful place from this day forward as the head of my life and come and live on the throne of my heart. Restore me to fellowship with you again and restore my seek. Let me make it a priority. Amen.

Lavished in Love

"Love never gives up, never loses faith, is always hopeful, and endures through every circumstance."–1 Corinthians 13:7 NLT

Sometimes, it's easy to give up on the people we love because we feel that they aren't going to get to the place we think they should be, or they don't look, act, or think like we want them to. I've been on both ends of this spectrum, and to be the one given up on isn't one of the greatest feelings or experiences. It'll leave you questioning why are you the way you are and are you really hard to love or worthy of love. Love is never about a feeling, but is often displayed through actions. Thankfully, God isn't like us. He never gives up on us. He proves His love time and time again through the things that He does to remind us of such a simple sentiment that we are loved. Whether it be to send a stranger to remind you, have a car with a cute bumper sticker pass by you, have a billboard light up, or even let something come across the TV or radio. God will go to the extremes to get to you. That is how you will know that you are lavished in love, because true love never gives up nor quits. You ever had that person who has had a serious crush on you for a while and won't stop pursuing you no matter how much you've communicated that the feelings aren't quite mutual or that you aren't quite ready? Yea? Well, God is just like that and He has been that to me. He showed me through the past few years that one thing that I am and always will be is lavished in love. I am lavished in love from God because He constantly pursues me no matter how much I run, retreat, or ignore Him. The enemy often times wants us to believe that we aren't enough and that God doesn't love us, when in fact, it's the complete opposite. In 2017, God changed my life and wrecked my world in ways that I couldn't imagine. I literally had a life-changing encounter with God that all worked for my good. God asked for my yes and I gave Him my yes, but what I didn't know was that what followed would lead to a few noes, I don't knows, and not yets. I was reading through the story of Jonah in the Bible and found myself in the pages ignoring God, running, hiding, in pursuit of my own agenda. Through all of the discomfort and uncertainty, even the painful experiences that blurred my vision and practically snatched my recollection of God's love for me, when the fog cleared, God helped me to look around and see that He never once gave up on me, and that I was surrounded in His love even with the presence of others in my life. Just as Jonah, there is nothing I will go through or encounter and no matter what someone tells me, no matter who comes into my life and leaves because they feel that I am not enough or that I am too much to love, God will always remain in pursuit of me as His daughter and bride. He will love me. When you're loved well you begin to glow up and act like it. Your attitude changes, your heart is not bleeding on others anymore; you're more confident in knowing that you are so loved that God has got you on this walk, and you learn to release all the pain, stress, worries, and cares to Him. Some days may get heavy and you may lose sight of the thought that God loves you, but breathe and look around, take in all that God is doing to remind you that you are loved. He is always gracious to send you some type of clue or reminder. You are too precious for Him to desert you and neglect or pull away His love. Another thing, when the love is real, you begin to operate in all that comes with it. You feel purposed.

Prayer: Father, thank you for loving me when I couldn't love myself, when others hurt me and made me feel unloved and too much to handle. Thank you for reminding me that nothing can separate me from your love, not even me running and retreating the other way, because you won't give up on me and will remain in constant pursuit of me. Thank you for allowing me to see and recognize the signs and things in my life that speak to the existence of your love in my life and remind me to settle into it and not run from me. Show me how to allow myself to be lavished in your love. Let my heart beat again and continue to beat for you, for life, and for others. Let me be a reminder of your love to someone else. Even when I run like Jonah, remind me that there's nowhere I can go from you because I will always be caught up in your love. As you are patient with me, kind to me, gentle with me, persistent, consistent, and protective with me, teach me to show up and be that for myself and allow others to do that when the love aligns with your biblical standards. Let me resolve that it is of you and it's ok to receive it. Then let me take what is poured into me and teach me to lavish others in the same love that aligns with your word. Let your love continue to pursue me and cover me in my mind, body, and soul. Amen.

Misfit

"Do not conform to the pattern of this world, but be transformed."– Romans 12:2 NIV

I wasn't born to fit in., I was born to stand out. I once despised being the sore thumb in the room, the one who'd go to the party and stand on the wall because I felt like I didn't belong, so I avoided parties at all costs. The one who in social settings agreed to have one, two… okay, maybe a few drinks and the next day, I felt convicted. The one who God gave crazy instructions to in her quiet time and tried to explain to everyone unknowingly that it was just for her and God to understand, or the girl who tried to settle for relationships that she knew God didn't call her to just to shut others up because they were questioning why she was waiting until marriage for sex. The girl who took a leap of faith and quit her job with no plan or other job lined up, the one who couldn't quite get into that song because the lyrics completely went against her values and standards God wanted her to uphold. I realized that all along, I wasn't a sore thumb in the room, but I'd always be misunderstood, because while I live in this world, I, too, am a dead woman walking. Christ now lives in me and I have a standard to uphold and convictions to live by. God doesn't hold us to this standard of perfection nor does He require us to get this walk right every day. There's grace for that, but there's a difference in pulling the grace card because you know it's there and absolutely needing to pull on that thing. While I live in this world, I am called to be different and be the difference that I want to see in the earth. God wants me to be about the Kingdom, and anything that goes against it can't stay nor stand, and I must live by that. While others will never understand and shun me for it, criticize me, or even joke on me, it's not always a bad thing, because what I'm doing wrong in their eyes is living right in God's eyes. When you give God that yes, you technically take a step of faith to step out and be the opposite, to be misunderstood, and that's absolutely ok. You no longer do what the world does in the ways the world does it. We see this in the word through various people that God used to be the opposite: Noah, Jonah, Abraham, Moses. God told them to take steps of faith, to do things in a different manner, defy the odds, and even do crazy things. You are not them and they are not you, so holdfast to your convictions and allow God to surround you by likeminded people who will get you and uphold the same standards. Lastly, when God tells you to say no, let your no be your no, and when He gives you a yes and tells you to say yes, let your yes be your yes. As long as you follow the convictions of your heart, God will guide you and lead you down the right path. The more you walk in relationship with Him, you'll want to continue going deeper with Him and learning His ways and what's best for you. This is in no way to shun anyone for what they are doing but to invite you into fellowship with Holy Spirit and communion with the Father so that you'll begin to walk, talk, and act more like Him. This may make the world not understand you and your thoughts, ways, and actions, but allows you the opportunity to introduce them to your Heavenly Father.

Prayer: Father, thank you for loving me so much that you sent your only son to die for my sins. Thank you for forgiving me of my sins and reminding me daily that this walk is about you and not me nor them. God, reveal to me the areas of my life that need change and help me to change them. Continue to let me see the standard that you want me to live by and uphold. Thank you for your grace and mercy each day that allows me to live in relationship with you and come back to you easily when I fall. Father, come into my heart, forgive me. I accept you as my Lord and Savior. Thank you for saving me from a life of sin, for freeing me so that I may live a life with you now and forever in eternity. Comfort me when I feel alone and when no one is there or understands. Continue to let me journey with you, knowing that you are right by my side at all times. Let me not forget your correction and conviction are from a place of love and not anger or condemnation. Don't let me allow the enemy to whisper that lie to me. Let me walk with you daily and set the standard for those even around me, and continue to send me likeminded people that we can grow together in you and teach others the standard. Let me not feel the need to shrink, be silent, or conform when it's not the popular opinion in the room, but let me grow in confidence and knowing that with following you and obeying you, I can't go wrong. As I leave or remove myself from things that don't align with your will, fill that void and empty space with more of you. Let transformation take root now, begin a new work in me and live in and through me. Amen.

Mediator

"Pray in the Spirit at all times and on every occasion. Stay alert and be persistent in your prayers for all believers everywhere."–Ephesians 6:18 NLT

You ever had someone constantly ask you for prayer every time you see them, or you have those sleepless nights where God lays some burden on your heart and wakes you at 3 am to pray for someone? Kind of like He did in this instance right now, where I'm up late at night interceding even for those I have never met or even spoken to. I may not always know you by name, but I flow with what Holy Spirit gives me. If I'm honest, there were nights where I was frustrated because I wanted to sleep until it was time to wake up and get ready for work. It was years of the late nights before I had language and understanding of what God was doing. God was showing me how to tap into the intercessory anointing on my life. There were some prayers I could pray to reach heaven on behalf of my brothers and sisters who may not know how to pray or even know what to pray, especially during those times where it seems like hell has sent an assault on their lives and they can't seem to get a prayer through or don't have insight of what's going on. I realized that I was called to intercept the plan of the enemy and stand in the gap as a mediator for my brothers and sisters, petitioning heaven on their behalf and praying off things that they didn't see but God gave me a glimpse of in the spirit. Sometimes, God will allow us to have a heavy burden to pray for someone or give us a prayer assignment by laying a general burden on our heart, not knowing that we are interceding over something through that burden. There is need of you and your voice. Your prayers carry some weight in the spirit and are necessary when others can't be there for themselves or forget to be there. You will literally be the one that God uses. You may be the missing link of heaven coming into agreement on someone's behalf, as God can give you the words to utter to heaven, especially when you are using your heavenly language. You may not know exactly what you are praying, but there's something about you praying in the spirit when Holy Spirit nudges you to do so or when Holy Spirit reveals something to you that you come into agreement with in prayer. When you are praying in your heavenly language, in doing so, that enemy is unaware of what you are praying. You have a one-up on Him. Let me encourage you: you don't have to have it all together to receive this infilling, just simply believe and allow God to flow to make the atmosphere conducive for Him. I did this at home years ago and God met me right where I was. Prayer became a heavy assignment on my life, which is why I also understand that it is the very thing I have to battle for, because there's something that takes place in the spirit realm and the natural realm. When I pray, chains break, change comes, shifts take place, literally nothing is the same, even my mindset is renewed. So I understand that one tactic the enemy uses is to keep me exhausted or distracted so that I don't find time to pray, because He is afraid of the outcome of what will happen when I do. There is a prayer warrior down on the inside of you that is stirred up and God pushes to release.

Prayer: Father, thank you for the ability to come into your presence once again today. I ask that you will fill me up again and allow me to be baptized by fire and let the gift of tongues come upon me so that I can counteract the enemy and his tactics in prayer as well as remain strengthened when he is trying to weaken me. Father, when I don't know what to say, give me the words to say and pray. Show me to lean on you in prayer and trust you with all of the outcomes, releasing myself from the pressure to perform or have things perfect. Father, show me how to take rest in you and flow with you through every prayer assignment that you place upon me. Let me not allow fear, laziness, or uncertainty to keep me from petitioning heaven on behalf of myself or others. Let me stand in the gap selflessly in prayer where needed. Give me strength even in the times where I experience early morning roll call. Give me a refreshing in your presence that I don't even miss or feel the time of rest I missed. Let me continue to pray without ceasing no matter what. Continue to strengthen my prayer muscles as I am obedient to the assignments. Remind me that no prayer goes in vain and they don't fall upon deaf ears. Continue to answer and let your glory be revealed, let your fire fall, let chains be broken, let miracles, signs, and wonders be released. Amen.

Motivator

"Encourage the fainthearted, help the weak, be patient with them all."– 1 Thessalonians 5:14 ESV

We all need a little encouragement and motivation at times. That is why I am personally thankful for my mentors, coaches, family members, and inner circle who do it willingly. I can be strong at times, but there's simply something that happens in me when I see others pushing through similar if not even tougher situations than I am going through and thriving, or when others whom I allow to get into the pit with me encourage me in the midst of the trials, tribulations, and trying times. I was facing a season in my career that seemed so dry, mundane, and pointless. I was beginning to show up to work late just because I was honestly losing interest and the feeling of purpose being fulfilled. Then, one day, God showed up. He allowed me to come in contact with a client who parted their lips to speak into me, who didn't even understand what they were doing at the time, thinking that they we were simply having a conversation, but their words were bringing me affirmation, encouragement, and essentially, healing. This person was dealing with a lot and told me that they were still living and pressing because of me. They felt that they had something to be happy about, keeping positivity at the forefront of their mind and day, and they felt that they had the strength to carry on longer. These words almost brought me to tears because they didn't understand that I was showing up to work down every day on the inside but with a smile on my face, and behind closed doors when I went home at night, I was crying out to God daily concerning my own life and situation. This person motivated me to keep pressing and living myself but helped me to see why I can't quit and how my life is a testimony and reassurance to others to keep them motivated to stay positive, press, praise, and pray their way through even the hardest situations or dry seasons of their lives. You may be working a job that seems pointless, living at home with your parents still as an adult, sleeping on a relative's couch, yet waking up with the motivation and drive to keep going, driving a car that's a few start-ups from breaking down, running a business that seems to not be bringing in any sales, trying to survive college with no money and little community, just to name a few. You may find yourself in some of these scenarios, or not, but I have and I know that God gave me strength and ability to press through, and while going through it all I remained able to motivate and encourage others to do the same. Because of you, someone is smiling, laughing, living, and enjoying their life still. Keep being that motivation that they need in life.

Prayer: Father, thank you for being my biggest fan and cheerleader, for seeing me through all of the hard times and trials that life throws me. Thank you for giving me grace to endure and the ability to do it with such grace that I can even motivate and encourage others to push through their tough times, knowing that they will make it out on the other side. Thank you for letting me inspire everyone I come in contact with in some way to keep going and never quit. Let me be able to testify of your goodness and how you pulled me through so that they'll know that they have a reason to push through and faith and hope that they will survive even the hardest seasons. Thank you for the reminder that nothing about our lives and situation is called to be mundane. You have use of it all and there's purpose in it all and everywhere that we are. Use it all for your glory. Amen.

Number One

"The fastest runner doesn't always win the race, and the strongest warrior doesn't always win the battle."–Ecclesiastes 9:11 NLT

I've always been one to love a good healthy competition, one where you can compete and laugh whether you lose or win. I wasn't so great at sports, but I joined the marching band where we competed often in national competitions and local competitions, some where we took home first place trophies, and others where we took home second place trophies. No one likes the thought of going in expecting first place and coming out in second place. I was driving down the road one day and the bulletin board read "second to none," and usually those words would sound snobby and as if one has their head in a cloud and has it all together. Well, that's what it could've been taken as, but God gave me a fresh revelation of that statement to remind me of a recent conversation I was having with some close friends concerning finding our lanes and thriving in purpose and how we've seen God's hand moving individually in each of us. God showed me how there were times where it seemed I was on consecration and in a season of rest and things were at a halt for me, whereas my friends were taking off. I could've taken offense to this and became jealous, envious, and grew angry with God, but I understood that we all had our own assignment and our own lane to walk in. It wasn't a race to see who could get to the finish line first, but rather, who could get there without quitting and doing fully what God was specifically telling them to do, thriving in their own lane. God showed me to never get lost in positions in this race because at the end of the day, you are second to none. There're no comparison games here; it's all about seasons, timing, and obedience in the kingdom. Knowing when to rest and when to go, when to be still and when to do something, when to leave and when to stay, acknowledging your individual instructions in and out of season. There have been times where I felt that God was speaking to me concerning my heart and other matters but when it came to purpose and instructions, man, was He fairly silent. Looking back now, I know why, because He loved me enough to not let me fall because of character, thinking that I had to rush my way to the top. I can truly look up now and say I'm right where God wants me and that I haven't missed a beat, including all those times of rest. You know why? It's because we serve a God who controls time and is able to even redeem the time He had you resting and call you out to the forefront, sometimes sooner than you think. That is currently my reality. God has been accelerating me and moving me into places and spaces I never could've imagined, and He can do the same for you. If you take the time to drop the offense and ideas of competition and comparison, you are who you are and you're right where God intended for you to be. You'll never lose your place in line if you run your race at the pace of His grace. He has graced each of us to run according to His timing and the season He has us in. Follow Him, don't run ahead of Him, and don't lag behind Him.

Prayer: Father, thank you for helping me to posture and position myself where you want me. Teach me to discern the season that you have me in. When it's time to rest, let me take rest; when it's time to go, let me go without hesitation; when it's time to speak, let me do so boldly; when it's time to consecrate and prepare for the next season, let me do so without putting up a fight. Teach me to genuinely support others in their good seasons and in their bad seasons, even if it's not the same season as mine. Thank you for affirming in me that this isn't a race on positions to the finish line but rather who can make it without quitting and by staying in step with you. Let me not grow jealous, envious, or offended when I don't get a blessing, promotion, or elevate at the same pace and timing of those around me. Teach me the pace of your grace that you have graced me to walk at with you and let me not lag behind you or run ahead of you. Show me when I am out of step or when my heart isn't right and let me correct it. Fix my sight and focus to be on you and not a title nor position. Help me to be confident in where I am in you and give me hope that I can trust that you hold the world and the time in your hands, and that you are the God who can redeem, elevate, and promote faster than anything I can do on my own or any place or position that anyone can give me. Thank you for the spirit of contentment in you resting upon me even now. Amen.

Nurturing

"He makes the barren woman to be a homemaker *and* a joyful mother of [spiritual] children. Praise the Lord!"–Psalms 113:9 AMPC

I was in a work meeting one day and we took a personality test. I love personality tests. Although they don't always get everything down to a "T," they are almost always pretty accurate. This test that I took reminded me that I was a helper, compassionate, and tend to lean more to things that call for me to nurture. I found this to be very true, especially in my professional life. I've always wanted to help out, give back, and take care of others from children to adults. I've always especially enjoyed being around little children and been intrigued by women who have a lot of children. They seem to brighten my day, especially those who show signs of silent screams in their eyes begging and pleading for someone to love on them and take care of them. At my current age, in my late 20s, society usually expects one to be married and have reproduced by now, but that isn't quite the story God had planned out for me. I actually struggled with the thought of ever parenting, so oddly, this was absolutely ok with me. From the recent rises of cases of women being infertile, having miscarriages, and losing children, honestly, I wrote myself off from ever wanting to experience any of it. Fear gripped my heart concerning mothering. Thoughts swam through my head like, would I even be a good mother to my children? What if I miscarried my baby? What if I had complications during labor and delivery? Or, what if I simply couldn't conceive? What I didn't realize was as fear was having a hold on me concerning natural birth, it also was doing some damage to me and my spiritual ability to nurture and birth something. God began to deal with me in this area and led me to begin to cover myself and my future children in prayer every time I felt a worry arise, but also to understand that being a mother doesn't define me. There will always be something that God calls us to birth and nurture. We as women are meant to have a nurturing touch whether it be to birth that book, ministry, workshop, conference, business, and even that child. Something I've personally come to realize is that you've got to be in the right environment and around the right people for your baby to leap. There's something in you lying dormant that's waiting to leap and for you to give birth to it. You are fertile and your womb shall produce in the spirit and the natural.

Prayer: Father, thank you for placing your creative and nurturing nature in me. Remind me that I haven't missed the mark of motherhood. Thank you for touching my womb even now and surrounding me with an Elizabeth, as you did for Mary, who will cause my baby to leap and begin to grow. Thank you for letting me free myself from society's standards and timelines on when I should give birth and teaching me to trust you and your timing. Thank you for the gift you've instilled in me to be able to produce and create and carry all of my babies' full term in both the spirit and the natural. When fear tries to grip my heart out of fear of aborting and miscarrying, remind me of your finished work on the cross that covered my every move. Thank you for letting me be fruitful in season and out of season, bearing good fruit. Teach me to lean on you when I'm tired and weary, rejuvenate me and bring me back to a place of sweet rest and restoration when the labor pains and contractions become a lot in the birthing process. I come against the spirit of death and the reports the enemy tries to send my way concerning me reproducing. I cancel it out under the blood and command life and good fruit to come forth from me. I proclaim that my baby won't just leap and stay incubated past time, but it will live and bless others. Let me see myself through your lens as a mother even before it comes to pass. Continue to help me protect, love, and cherish what you give me but offer it back to you also. I pray that infertility and barrenness will no longer define me as a woman or keep me from living the life you called me to. Flip my story and use my testimony for your glory. Amen.

Orator

"Let the words of my mouth, and meditation of my heart, be acceptable in thy sight, O Lord, my strength and my redeemer."–Psalms 19:14 KJV

Sometimes we run from the call of God on our lives and for many years, I did just that. Being in the cave, remaining muzzled when God was asking me to speak, write, encourage, pray, and teach others. One thing I learned was that God wanted me to be His mouthpiece, to say what He was transmitting through me into the earth and lives of others. Words that could bring healing, breakthrough, deliverance, and language to someone's heart, mind, life, and future. I realized I was a quiet storm hidden in plain sight, called upon occasionally but when the time came, I was able to allow God to use me to speak life, to speak the things that He was calling me to speak, to shake up rooms and bring about change. As I speak, I have the ability through Christ to use the words that He gives me to motivate, encourage, inspire, intercede, prophecy, teach, and most importantly, to love. Throughout college, I dropped a public speaking class multiple times, running in fear of speaking in front of others. I loved writing and journaling, but when it was time to present openly, it was a No for me. It was kind of the same with this book. Many of these ideas sat for a while, then things began to unfold over time and God gave me everything to put on this page to speak into your life. You, too, have that same power to be the mouthpiece and voice for God to speak and bring about change, to love, inspire, motivate, and encourage.

Prayer: Father, give me the wisdom to know what to say, how to say it, and when to say it. Teach me to keep myself at your feet and seek wisdom from you so that I may keep my gift submitted to you. Father, let the words of my heart bring about change, healing, wisdom, encouragement, inspiration, motivation, and life to others who are tuned in and receiving what you have to say. Father, let me never jump ahead of you or get lost in the approval and applause of others, nor let me grow offended when I am not received as I think I would be. Let me remain quiet and hidden until you reveal me and want me to come forth. Let no words spoken or released go in vain or fall upon deaf ears. Let me continue to consult you when I am doing things and even on behalf of how to handle others with care. Remind me that playing small and silent doesn't serve others well because they may need to experience healing, breakthrough, and deliverance. Let the meditation of my mouth forever be acceptable in your sight. Continue to let me stay submitted to you as you reveal your hidden knowledge for my life and others. Let me speak only that in which you give me to say. Let me roar like a lion and chase off demons, giants, and anything sent to stop, hinder, or kill that which is attached to me in any way, whether it be friends, family, or strangers. Let me continue to live as your spokesman when you instruct me to and let my words be seasoned with love and grace. Above anything, use me, Lord. I'll be the one. Let fear no longer hold me captive and keep me on mute or blinded to the things I am called to speak out on and for, and people I am called to speak to. Amen.

Poised with Tenacity

"When you go through rivers of difficulty, you will not drown. When you walk through the fire of oppression, you will not be burned."– Isaiah 43:2 NLT

There's a reason He gave me this specific word. I learned the word *tenacious* a few years ago and basically, it is defined as "persistence while poised, to remain composed, dignified, and unwavering." When I think of this posture, I think of how life often deals us various cards with different circumstances that we experience and has a way of altering us in our words, actions, thoughts, and the posture of our hearts at times. I've dealt with some things such as rejection, abandonment, financial struggles, depression, sleeping on an air mattress and couches while riding around with clothing in my car, as well as experiencing having an incarcerated parent, just to name a few. I sometimes think that this was life's way of putting me in the classroom and teaching me some things, building my spiritual muscles, faith, and stretching me to test how tenacious, indestructible, and poised I'd remain through it all, because for some, having to deal with some tough situations has a way of making them grow angry, bitter, calloused and they check out on life and others. I, on the other hand, thank God for showing me tips and tools to surviving it all with Him and that he has allowed me to never have to turn my heart on Him or others regardless of how bad it hurts. He has taught me to remain in Him and be still. He has graced me for some of the things I've dealt with, and none of them were able to take me out or take me under. They made me who I am today and I thank

Him for the ability to remain so confident in Him that nothing can shake my faith. Lately, I've found that I was receiving compliments that didn't make sense at the time but as I reflected on them, they did. I had things told to me like, "You look so happy now," "You're glowing," and "You always remain positive," when in actuality, I experienced a season of the complete opposite. I was depressed, crying myself to sleep every night, hibernating in a dark room. I'd literally put on a fake smile long enough to leave the house between 9-5. I couldn't see the light, I was losing hope, and it seemed like I was slipping off the deep end, but something changed in me. I can't quite explain it, but I know that it was nothing but an encounter with God that gave me that true happiness and Jesus' glow. God showed me that the trials will come but despite those difficulties I encounter, that I had access to power, love, and a sound mind, and that one thing for sure is, I will never be overtaken. I can and will always have love, laughter, and life. I'll never be moved but stay graciously seated regardless of what comes and what goes.

Prayer: Father, thank you for allowing me to remain poised in my seat, unshaken and unmoved by the trials and tribulations that come my way. Teach me to tap into the tenacious spirit you have placed within me to be resilient in spite of, to keep pressing and fighting. Show me how to not allow my circumstances to define me and how I feel or operate, but let me have the ability to overcome and keep going even in the midst. Let me keep my composure and may my posture in the kingdom as a daughter always remain the same. Nothing that I experience is a surprise to you. Let me know that I can come to you for wisdom on how to go through it and get to the other side. God, show me how to guard my heart so that life will always flow from it and that I'll never grow angry, bitter, or hard hearted due to what has come my way or even what others have said or done to me. Let me allow you to cover me and keep my heart flowing in love and giving off life. Father, show me how to continuously forgive and not be moved by the words, opinions, and even negativity of others. When depression comes and tries to overtake me, show me how to continue to find my strength and joy in you. Restore my laughter and singing. Let the hurts and pains be covered by your love. Today I choose to shake off the grave clothes and rely on you for strength to keep living. I won't give up on life or be moved. I have life and I will continue to live. Depression cannot have me or claim my life. I will no longer live in survival mode but live, thrive, and soar. Amen.

Quality

"She is worth far more than rubies."–Proverbs 31:10 NIV

There was truly a point in life where I didn't see my value. I didn't understand my worth, especially having word curses spoken over me, telling me lies that I wasn't anything and would never be anything and had nothing to offer. These words shattered me and my perception of myself. I found myself beginning to believe each of these lies despite the fact that my mother had drilled in me and my siblings' heads that we were somebody and no one could take that from us. My inability to not be able to see my worth caused me to settle for less in so many areas of my life, later on bringing about guilt, shame, and much regret, causing me to waste time on the woulda, shoulda, coulda. I lost sight of who I was in Christ and how valuable I was to Him and in this world. In fact, He came in and healed those wounds and allowed me to see myself through His lens to see that I was literally worth dying for. What better way to prove to someone that they are worth all that and some, or as some say, "all that and a bag of chips." I was literally to die for. I was and am worth loving. I have so many valuable aspects to my life and existence that He sees fit to have me here every day to do His work, to love on people, and to be the light to the surrounding darkness. Some people say leave your valuables at home to protect them, but I don't have to worry about that because God has me protected and insured. That's how valuable I am. There are valuable things inside of me that He has hidden for due season, but He saw fit to entrust me with. You may be like me and enjoy thrifting. Some don't appreciate the art of thrifting because they believe that the clothing is cheap and no good, but in actuality, there are times I leave the store with some signature statement pieces for my closet, some of which still have tags on them and others worth so much in the stores, and me understanding that they are such quality pieces even though I got them at a cheaper price was a sign that this, too, is how God sees me. That no matter what I've gone through or where I've come from or where I stray to, He has the power and ability to use me and place me where needed, and He sees beyond what I see and what others see. He sees a daughter who is worth far more precious that rubies. A daughter who was worth laying down His life for. A daughter who has purpose, who can be used, and is an asset to the world and a liability to the kingdom of hell because of the damage she can do.

Prayer: Father, thank you for reminding me of who I am in you. Heal me of the regrets, guilt, and shame that I've allowed to take place in my heart and mind due to me settling for less. Remind me that you are a God who forgets and forgives and teach me to forgive myself and move forward in my new knowledge of who I am in you and never settle another day. Remind me that I am not my past nor my mistakes and those things don't define who I am in you. Show me how to walk, talk, and be more like you and operate in the power that you've given me to do damage to the kingdom of hell. Reassure me when I forget how valuable I am and how I am an asset to the kingdom of God and a liability to the kingdom of hell, that you thought I was worth dying for, saving, investing in, and using daily. Thank you for entrusting me with all that you have given me. When I look in the mirror from this day forward, allow me to only come into agreement with what you speak over me and see what you see, and that is a Daughter of the King who is an asset worth far more than the pricey rubies the world has to offer.

I come out of agreement with all word curses spoken over me and allow the words of life and love to flood my wounds and remind me of my position, authority, and power in you. When I forget and allow others to not see my worth, teach me to not grow bitter, angry, or offended that they don't see who I am in you and how much I am worth. Teach them to see their worth and help them to be healed to learn to see the worth in others. Show me how to maneuver and go where I am appreciated, celebrated, and allowed to be unapologetically me. Amen.

Quiet Storm

"A time to keep silent; and a time to speak."–Ecclesiastes 3:7 AMP

One thing about me that you've probably learned throughout this book is that I absolutely love science and figuring out the "why" behind things. It was one of my favorite subjects in school. It was only right for God to reveal to me that I was a quiet storm. You heard of the saying "the calm before the storm"; that's usually me. The quiet, shy girl in the room capable of shaking up the atmosphere and bringing about a change when the time comes. Storms generally come abruptly after a calm moment, and they generally come unannounced, when you least expect it, and did I mention many storms are pretty dangerous and can cause damage? Thunderstorms take time to form but once they come, there's no going back. They come for everything in their path, that's thunderstorms, ice storms, tornados, floods, dust storms, and hail storms. Storms have a way of blowing your mind with showing the power that they have and damage they can cause. Precautions are typically necessary when dealing with a storm. I, too, realized that I had this characteristic, although I disliked people looking at me as the quiet girl in the room when I knew there was more down within me and that I had some power and could do some damage—not in the violent sense but definitely in general and in the spirit. I realized I was like a secret weapon who God had on reserve. He allows things to build up in me over periods of time and then suddenly, boom, He allows me to go in and shake up rooms where needed. I've learned to appreciate being this quiet storm that others least expect, just as the story of David. Newsflash, God has a way of choosing and using the least expected to do some things to take over the position to occupy the room to be the leader, or whatever the case may be. God doesn't always pick the one people would think is the fastest, most qualified, smartest, loudest, or strongest. If you're introverted or afraid or feeling inadequate, may I encourage you today to embrace that quiet storm within you. Don't waste another day looking at yourself as just this quiet person. While that may be a part of your personality and who you are, might I suggest to you it's not all that you are. You have many layers and there're more parts of you to be revealed to the world over time. Allow God to continue to use you. If He chooses you for it, you are far more than capable to enter a room and shake it up, and that doesn't mean you have to yell and be loud, you can simply change the atmosphere, change someone's thought process, or even bring about new systems and ideas. Keep embracing every layer of you and letting God use you.

Prayer: Father, thank you for allowing me to accept every part of who you've made me to be and not try to change that. Father, thank you for building up within me the stamina, increasing the anointing and power, and causing me to go into rooms and do what you tell me to do, say what you tell me to say, and be where you want me to be. Let me cause there to be a change in every room that my feet enter, may no one leave my presence the same because they've had an encounter with you through me. Thank you for allowing me to remain quiet until you tell me to speak and when you tell me to speak, let me not sit back in fear and forfeit that assignment for which you have placed me in the room to do. Father, thank you for letting minds be changed and letting the narrative shift for me because of their encounter with you through me. Thank you that wherever I go, systems will be changed and I will leave no room or space untapped. Give me the boldness, confidence, and courage to go forth in you and know that I have the power to overtake everything that has ever tried or will try to overtake me. Show me that the storm within me that operates through Holy Spirit's empowerment is bigger than any storm I will ever encounter or that is taking place around me. Amen.

Resilient

"We are afflicted in every way, but not crushed; perplexed, but not driven to despair; persecuted, but not forsaken; struck down, but not destroyed."–2 Corinthians 4:8-9 ESV

Growing up in church my whole life, I thought I really knew God and had it going on. One day, I had this urging hunger and deep longing for more. I laid on the couch watching a sermon, then shortly after picked up the Word and decided to have a look in it for myself outside of the typical Sunday morning sermon. I flipped open the book to Job and was fairly intrigued by the story and all that he went through and how God restored him. Now, what I didn't know was that wasn't just me reading any old random Bible story, but God sending me encouragement and preparation for what I was about to endure over the next few years: a place called the wilderness, just like Job. I am thankful for this place now more than I was when I was in it. This was the place where God did some pruning, purging, and stretching beyond my imagination. Everything I once knew before was no longer, and every crutch that I had was gone, but what I didn't realize was that something was happening in me. God was bringing out the warrior within, the warrior who refused to throw in the towel and quit just because life had gotten hard. God was showing me that I was resilient and that He was just equipping me to be a skilled warrior for any other battles I'd ever face, showing me how to fight back in the spirit and put on my armor. He taught me how to overcome some things that would take others out and even cause them to turn away from Him.
Meanwhile, I grew in my faith and even found my praise. God showed me during this season that Goliaths will come but I am a skilled warrior

to take them all down one stone at a time. Nothing that I went through was ever to just experience pain or in vain just to know what it's like to go through, but to get the resilient, skilled warrior in me to arise and shine for the battle.

Prayer: Father, thank you for using everything that I've gone through to strengthen and stretch my spiritual muscles. Thank you for showing me the strength that lied within me and teaching me to never quit nor give up on the fight. Thank you for your reminders that no matter what comes my way, I can't be crushed, and even as Isaiah 43:2 says, I can't drown. I may be in up to my neck, but you'll always come to my rescue. Thank you for saving me from my despair, from sorrow, defeat, trials, and restoring me to a place of joy and sweet rest. Give me patience to withstand the battle when it gets long and hard. Teach me to lean and depend on you more in the trying times. Allow the resilient and skilled warrior in me to arise and take her rightful place. Teach me how to fight and not just fight, but give me strategy on the right weapons to use to attack and slaughter what's trying to attack, suffocate, and kill me. Thank you for the wilderness being my place of growth and the place that launches me into my next level. Let me not run from it but hold on tighter to you in it and listen more closely for your voice and instructions. Amen.

Resourceful

"She selects wool and flax and works with eager hands. She is like the merchant ships, bringing her food from afar, she gets up while it is still night, she provides for her family and portions for her female servants."–Proverbs 31:13-15 NIV

On multiple occasions, God gave me some silly instructions to leave my job and do XYZ. I could never quite wrap my mind around why He would select me for such a task and honestly didn't feel that I could do it. One of the times where I left, I was home for a few days and began going on a downward spiral. The enemy had me believing that God was trying to embarrass me or that I didn't hear Him clearly and jumped prematurely. God sent someone my way to speak life into my situation and what was happening at the time. I wasn't getting selected for any of the new jobs I was applying for and nothing was coming through. You know why? Because God was trying to stretch my faith in Him and show me that there was so much more in me that needed to come out, but it would take some digging, some praying, some planning, and some steps of faith in producing. God was trying to show me that even though I had little, honestly, cashing checks that barely covered all of my bills wasn't cutting it, and trying to remain faithful in tithing, I was growing weary. God was trying to get me to see that with the little I had I was being stretched and challenged to invest and use what I had in front of me. Sometimes God requires us to use what we have and He will do the honors of stretching it. There are many occasions in the word where a person was asked what they had and they'd answer nothing, but yet the story always ended in them making a small investment with what they had, offering it unto God as a sacrifice and being multiplied and miracles breaking out right before their eyes. Take the two fish and five loaves, for instance, that fed many and they had some leftover. Sometimes there're things hidden in us and in near sight that we just have to tap into and make use of, being the resourceful woman that He has called us to be, allowing Him to take what we offer and multiply it and increase it. I have a prayer list on my grandmother's refrigerator that I sowed a seed over and am still watching God bring to pass. There're principles to this equation of receiving. Giving + hard work + practicality + obedience + diligence to God + a pure heart = resources and fruit.

Prayer: Father, thank you for entrusting me to steward over all that you have assigned to me in the natural and in the spiritual realm. Thank you for teaching me to abide by your principles of giving and not being afraid to lose the little that I have. Allow me to have the ability to relinquish it to you and offer it diligently and with a pure heart. Search me and see that I am doing things with the right motives. Teach me that when I feel that there is a lack, you are more than enough and you are my provider. Thank you for showing me how to take what I have and use it and invest it to get what I need. Remove all laziness and complacency from me that wants to settle for mediocre and teach me to have a drive to reach the goals that you have given me, even when faced with opposition. God, let me dig deep and tap into the untapped well on the inside of me that will flow over into every area of my life. Let me not only be fruitful and multiply, but now show me how to invest and finance the kingdom through my resources. Thank you for showing me strategy and how to use what I have in the right manner.

Let me not grow weary in well doing and in the building and growing process but to keep putting in what I'd like to get out. Amen.

Sheltered

"There will be a shelter to give shade from the heat by day, and refuge and protection from the storm and the rain."– Isaiah 4:6 NASB

Growing up, I was what many would say was sheltered. I was protected by my family, couldn't do or say much that those around could or were doing, but as time went on, it seemed that this sense of security and shelter was pretty shaken. Moving away to college, getting my own apartment, experiencing some turbulence in family dynamics, especially when I experienced a long season of uncertainty, sleeping over friends' houses on blow-up mattresses, and riding around with clothing in my trunk and storage, praying to God that this never got out to anyone. I didn't know what God was doing in that season, and I honestly wanted to hide under a rock. I grew frustrated thinking that God wasn't hearing me or seeing me, afraid that I'd be homeless or that I was being a burden to others. I allowed shame and guilt to slip in that maybe I'd heard God wrong or took some wrong turns in life, or that maybe I just should end my friendships and relationships so no one could see this ugly portion of my life. That season was tough. I spent endless nights crying myself to sleep. I'd smile and not tell anyone. Eventually, God healed me of this lie and helped me to know that there were people out there for me who cared and weren't there to judge me, but most importantly, although I had to experience sleeping on a blow-up mattress in the corner of my grandmother's living room or ask a friend to sleep over at their house while taking clothes to and from with me often, I came to realize that not once did I have to sleep outside or in an abandoned house or on the street. God had me covered, and during this season, He was teaching me some things about myself, working in me more compassion for others, pushing me out of my comfort zone (literally uprooting my life and making me move to a new state). He was dealing with my ability to be vulnerable with those close to me and bringing healing to that area of my life. Lastly, He was reminding me that although it appeared that I was lacking things, I never lacked that shelter in the natural or in Him when the storms came. My natural life was a reflection of what He was proving to me in the spirit. It may seem uncertain, it may require some changes and shifts, it may require some work and movement on my behalf, but God will always have me covered. God has a way of keeping us covered, and even if we lose everything, we'll never lose Him and that protection.

Prayer: Father, I thank you for your constant reminders of your protection and ability to shelter me from the storms, rain, and pain. Keep me and cover me as you promised. Allow me to not place my eyes on my situation and circumstances so much that I miss out on this truth. Thank you for providing and meeting my every need, even those that I don't bring to you. Remind me that you know what they are and will provide. Thank you for the seasons of discomfort that caused me to experience more growth. Allow me to use it to testify to others of your goodness and ability and willingness to come and see about me. Thank you for allowing one thing to always remain: that you are my strength, rock, redeemer, and safe place, and in you I have safety and shelter both in the natural and the spirit. Break off the curse of poverty and homelessness and allow me to experience wealth and abundance to even be able to provide for others what they may stand in need of. I not only cover myself in this moment but all of those battling with homelessness or that feel that their world has been shaken up and has become uncertain. Bring about a peace and allow them to experience safety and security again. Send the right people their way and the resources and assistance that they need. Even allow their lives to reflect this in the spirit realm. Amen.

Surrounded

"You have surrounded me on every side, behind me and before me, and you have placed your hand gently on my shoulder."–Psalms 139:5 The Voice

Have you ever sat in a room that was full of people yet still experienced an emptiness down on the inside of you, almost as if no one was in the room with or even literally sitting beside you? Well, I have many times. I've been surrounded by others and felt completely alone. This feeling would happen often too. In 2019, God spoke to me on healing me of my rejection issues and showing me real love. Little did I know that He would begin to manifest this promise swiftly. God took this woman who was once a little shy girl who steered away from the crowds and stayed to herself, and began to put her in rooms and spaces where she had no space to isolate or run from the Love of God. She couldn't deny the fact that the girl that was once alone was now always engulfed and surrounded and a true recipient of God's love. I was once hanging around with some friends, having conversation about if we had a word to describe what God is to us, what would it be? For me, that word was a blanket. I felt that God always had my back and that He always had me covered no matter what. When I was in one of the toughest seasons of my life from 2017 to about 2018, I felt like I had no one to turn to during that time. But God, as I reflect on that season, I realize that nothing that I experienced during that time was able to take me out. Even if I was going through a wilderness season, God was with me and had me surrounded. One thing I truly love about God is how he operates in ways we don't even understand or would think. During that same time period, He slowly but surely began to bring people into my life who had language for my future. Ones who would go to war in prayer with me and for me. God showed me that I didn't have to do life alone and that He had me surrounded even in my relationships. He literally attached an agenda to those relationships and began to work through them to do something inside of me. I, in return, am able to now be that for others, to help be God's assistant, to remind them that they don't have to do life alone and that they are surrounded. God is a loving and protecting Father. Don't ever allow the enemy feed you those whispering lies that you are alone, God isn't with you and has forgotten about you, or that you have to do life alone, because you don't. It's all a lie and in due time, God will prove for you just as He did for me.

Prayer: Father, thank you for those gentle, loving reminders of your presence always being with me. Thank you for keeping me surrounded from all hurt, harm, and danger no matter what the enemy tries to throw my way. Keep me in your care and under your protection. When I begin to isolate and feed into the lies of the enemy that I am alone, lead me to your Word and truth that you are with me and will never allow anything to happen to me. Thank you for caring for my mind, body, and soul, and also for my emotions and knowing that I am human and made for relationships. Thank you for the God-sent, divine connections that you are stocking my life with now. Allow me to recognize them and receive them when they come and not self-sabotage or run out of fear or past comforts of loneliness and isolation. Remind me that this is simply another tactic the enemy wants to use to keep me stuck. Continue to take my hand and allow me to grip yours to walk with you on this journey as you guide me through. Keep me covered, blanket me in your protection, care, and love. Heal whatever is in me that needs to learn to receive you as ABBA, as my protector, as my shield, my anchor, and my solid rock who has me surrounded. Amen.

Tomb Raider

"He brought me up out of a pit of destruction, out of the miry clay, and He set my feet upon a rock making my footsteps firm."–Psalms 40:2 NAS

When you're called to be a soul snatcher for Christ, some days seem unbearable on your heart, being surrounded by many people whose souls have seemingly been snatched by the enemy. Looking at these people, you can almost see past them and what they are displaying on the outside, covering up with a nice, beautiful smile or many other things. You can hear the silent screams of despair, hurt, hopelessness. You can sense that they are muzzled and have lost their voice or are too weak to speak. They are seemingly tangled in the snares of sin and feel like they are gripped so tight that they are captured to no point of return. I was once of them that the enemy had trapped in cycles, silenced, hurt, and bound. People would often pray over me and call me out of the pits and caves that I didn't know that I was in. There were times I had reached my wits' end and was on the verge of giving up on my faith, calling, relationships, and even finding my voice. I wanted to lie down and die. God supernaturally began to pull me up and out, and each time I slipped back in, He'd send another to snatch me out. I've always disliked funerals and grave yards because my heart grieved for the souls that were lost and possibly didn't make it or died in their despair. Even hearing stories of suicide and suicidal attempts would shatter me. God began to show me why I was so amazed at how He pulled me out of my low places and used His servants to call me out of caves, graves, and pits and has need of me to do the same. God comes and saves us so that we can be the light to others in the darkness and teach them solutions and reassure them of the hope, joy, new life, and salvation that can be found in Christ. I learned that I didn't have to be a Bible scholar, prophet, or even intercessor to do these things. I just had to be open and available, and God would lead and guide me in my interactions on how to show love and call them up and out in a way that speaks to them and their need. Many souls are counting on both me and you to come in and snatch them out, to raid the tombs that they lie in dying. Areas where we see death every day, God is waiting for us to show up and raid the tombs to resuscitate some things to life.

Prayer: Father, thank you for giving me the boldness and the courage to go and raid tombs just as your servants have once done for me. Thank you for letting me see people beyond what they display and letting me see the hurt, pain, and snare of the enemy that is keeping them silenced and choking the life out of them. Allow me to call them up and out of the pits and graves that they have settled into. Thank you for a supernatural grace and anointing when encountering them that will allow me to bear their burdens and help reassure them of their place in the earth. Teach me what to say and do when reassuring them of your love, hope, and ability to restore and bring them back to life. Father, let me not quit in my pursuit to go to war for the lost souls, hopeless souls, and weary souls. Thank you for helping me to stand firm in seeing them snatched out from the pits, graves, and caves and rescued from hell's grasp. Let me not sit and watch anyone die that you've given me the access and ability to reach and go into the tomb and raid it. Let me continue to motivate, encourage, inspire, and pray myself and others through their mess. Father, let me see chains broken, muzzles removed, souls freed, people healed and delivered, walking upright and into all that you have called them to, snatching other souls along the way. Teach me and everyone I come in contact with to tap into the tomb raider in us, and let until all have heard, be our standard we uphold to bringing souls to the kingdom. Amen.

Torch Carrier

"One generation shall praise thy works to another and shall declare thy mighty acts."–Psalms 145:4 KJV

There are some people out there literally waiting to follow your lead. They are waiting for you to pick up the torch and get into position to guide them to where they need to go. One day I entered my apartment complex and headed to the elevator to go up to my floor. Upon me pressing the elevator button, there was a woman older than myself that came behind me and informed me that she had been waiting for someone to come and go on the elevator ahead of her, so that she would feel safe getting to her apartment that evening. As she exited the elevator and I continued to head to my floor, I was in awe thinking of the millions doing the same in my life, waiting for me to come in and pick up the torch to lead them. I've always had leadership qualities and been deemed as the eldest in many of my positions, especially in my family, being the oldest child and grandchild. With many others following in your footsteps, you learn those leadership qualities early. You learn to speak differently, behave differently, and do things that will set an excellent example for those coming behind you. Over time, life began to cause me to shy away into a corner and follow others, never really seeing myself as a leader anymore, but God reminded me that there are some things I want to see happen and that need to happen that will only come to pass by me stepping up and taking my place and role as a trailblazer, allowing God to use me to be the blueprint for others. Some people have no vision and need your guidance and leadership skills to get them unstuck. Then, on the other hand, there as tasks that maybe were assigned to others that fell on you, due to them going incomplete, and God has to call you to step up and get it done. There's some things in you that were meant to come from others, but it now has to come from you, and that's absolutely ok. Pick up the torch, put on the mantle, and allow God to get out of you what He needs to bring into the earth through you. This is a good time to evaluate and ask God where have you dropped the torch or simply haven't picked it up and decided to run yet. Some lives and generations are counting on you, torch carrier. They can't go unless you go, they can't do unless you do, they can't show up and be unless you show up and be. Trailblazing can be quite a task, especially when you are the blueprint, but you've got to learn to trust that God has got you and will guide you in being the one to carry the torch. Never let age or capabilities shut you down and make you insecure to feel that you are called, chosen, or qualified enough to carry that torch. Do what God says do willingly, and unto Him, He'll take care of the results and outcomes, just continue to walk with Him and allow that torch to light the trail way for others. There will be times where you'll have to do uncommon things or things that haven't been done. God will call you to step out and start a business, write a book, launch a program, relocate, and do things that others can't or won't do, but because of your willingness and obedience, many will be blessed.

Prayer: Father, thank you for choosing me to carry some torches, blaze some trails, and serve as a blueprint that will bless others. Show me the way you said in your word in Psalms 119:105, that your word is "a lamp unto my feet and a light to my path." Guide me in everything that I set out to do, and may it prosper. Father, forgive me for the assignments I have neglected and allow me to see myself through your lens as one who is called to lead and guide others in the directions that you have called them. Father, protect me in times of uncertainty and continue to keep me covered. Show me the blueprint and let me obey and do what you called me to do. Let me not neglect or leave behind anyone you are sending my way to lead. Teach me to believe in myself and no longer shrink to the room or shy in the corner. Let me arise to the occasion every time and accept the challenges you present to me, knowing that you will be right there to grace me to help others through. May the light of the torch that I carry burn the path ablaze for others. Teach me to no longer allow comparison to others to keep me stuck or stifled, but let me even feel big when it means taking risks. Show me to follow you as I lead others. Help me to remain decided that I will walk with you on this journey. Amen.

Unlabeled

"For the Lord sees not as man sees: man looks on the outward appearance, but the Lord looks on the heart."–1 Samuel 16:7 ESV

Every morning while getting ready for school, my mother would make my brothers and I stand in front of the mirror and scream at the top of our lungs and repeat multiple times, "I am somebody and can't nobody take that away from me." This affirmation stuck with me for the rest of my life, so much so that I still recite it to this day and said it loudly as I was writing this. The words hit way different now, as then I was just doing what I was told, but never realized that it was taking root in my heart all along, and eventually, words of affirmation became one of my biggest love languages. Words of affirmation being my love language had its pros and cons, because God began to surround me with people who literally spoke the words from the Father's heart concerning me, and He'd often speak to me through signs, books, songs, and other avenues Himself. But can I just remind you of just how sneaky the enemy is? He took some time to study me, including what I loved and responded to, and used that very same avenue to begin to have people speak negativity over me, telling me I was a nobody and that I had nothing going for me. In all honesty, I began to inspect my life and believe it. I slowly began to shut down, become depressed, and lose hope in areas of my life. During the Christmas holiday, while ordering some packages, God used me buying gifts to bring up old wounds and began to heal me in that area. Some boxes were beat up by the time they arrived, and others had some of the prettiest packaging. One thing I came to learn was it wasn't about the labels or packaging, but the value and what was inside. What I saw on the outside was always fairly different from what was on the inside. What was inside was valuable and quite pricey and often in plain old, brown cardboard box. We often heed to the warning that if the label or seal is broken or tampered with, then it's void and basically means nothing and holds no value, but it doesn't work like that in the kingdom of God. Broken is the way with God. He's able to take those broken parts and mend us for use. He often gets the best use of us when we come to Him in a state and posture of humility and brokenness. Just because you're broken doesn't mean you are labeled void, invalid, or to be counted out. In fact, it's not even about the labels that you or others have placed on you, but it's about what God has permanently stamped on you and calls you that you come into agreement with and begin to see yourself as such. As you do so you'll be more liberated, joyous, and feel powerful and full of purpose, no longer identifying with those false labels. You are not the negative words that they've spoken to you and over you. You are everything that God calls you plus some. Find value in that and add some taxes to it. You are more than enough. They can't even put you in a box and define you by one thing because God calls you many things. He sees your heart and knows your worth way more than any man or woman ever will. I encourage you to identify the false labels placed on you and snatch them off. Replace them with who God says that you are and begin to walk, talk, and act like it. Don't waste another day believing in that imposed false identity or focusing in so much on your brokenness that you're missing out on your value. Lastly, it's never about revenge. I feel led to share this because sometimes, when people call us names and speak things over us, we become so hurt that we allow bitterness and anger to grow because they can't see our worth or they didn't give us the label or title we wanted. It's ok: feel what you feel because your feelings are valid, but then you've got to release them to God. Let me tell you, the very people who talked down on me, God allowed them to watch me grow and elevate and come back to me for advice or with some kind words. This may not always be the case, but the biggest point is to shred the labels and release the offense from your heart.

Prayer: Father, thank you for helping me to identify with who and what you say that I am. Remove the anger, hurt, bitterness, and offense from my heart that has taken root towards those who have said negative things and done wrong towards me. Teach me to love them through it and allow you to handle my battles. Father, thank you for making my vision clear where it has been distorted concerning my identity, my purpose, and my future. Rip the labels and replace them with new ones. Continue to affirm me and uplift me when I need it most so that I may help other sisters rip their false labels and uplift them too. I know that I must first deal with me in order to help them. God, where my original labels and identity have been tampered with, restore them to factory settings prior to the false labels being placed on me. Remove the scales off of my eyes and give me the words of healing to speak over my sisters to remove the scales off of their eyes. Help me only to release words of positivity. Continue to bless those who curse me and let them see you and know you so they'll even learn themselves and stop harming others. Let the words of positivity that you, others, and myself speak over me take root in my heart again. Amen.

Unleashed

"For freedom Christ has set us free; stand firm therefore, and do not submit again to a yoke of slavery."–Galatians 5:1 NIV

Unleash Her has become of my favorite sayings because it was a God-given vision a few years ago. God literally began to give me words such as depression, insecurity, bitterness, suicide, brokenness, fear, pride, pornography, masturbation, lust, poverty, isolation, generational curses, addition, and soul ties. Things that God was revealing that He wanted to see His women set free from—myself included—as we are His daughters and He is very much concerned with the chains that the enemy has kept us bound to for so long. While you may not always relate with all of these, you've encountered some connection you've had to experience freedom and deliverance from physically, mentally, spiritually, or even emotionally. I personally have through a series of things such as prayer and deliverance at church, taking practical steps, community, accountability, and even currently seeking certified professionals such as therapists to talk to. Our freedom is contingent upon our willingness to be free and allow Holy Spirit to invade those areas of our lives. Sometimes we hide the ugly stuff, thinking that God can't handle those things, or we don't want to expose ourselves because the enemy lies to us about the guilt, shame, and condemnation that will come with it, when the word encourages us to allow God and others into those spaces and testify in order to be free. As I was writing this particular piece, I reflected on how I am sitting in the exact same place that I was sitting in eight years ago to this date, but now I have a new attitude, mindset, and courage to be me, and I've allowed Holy Spirit to invade so many areas in my life that being bound no longer makes since because He lives in my heart. I laughed and almost wanted to question God why I felt that there were still just a few cycles repeating themselves in my life, and He showed me how not to see them as negative but as the way that He keeps the thorn in my side to keep me near Him and coming to Him concerning them. These things strengthen my prayer and devotion time, and keep me accountable to God and others as I testify of the freedom He has brought me through, and now lead a ministry geared towards seeing other women free. He showed me how I must first walk in my freedom and own it to help others do the same. Over the course of writing this book, this was a big healing and deliverance process for me. I thought I was just being obedient and writing a book, but clearly, I needed it before you even got your hands on it. As I wrote more and more, I began to testify more and share pieces of me with others. This brought freedom to me and to them as well. There was a newness that came upon me, and God began to open new doors, new opportunities began to arise, and even new people and new possibilities, one of which being writing this book. When God revealed to me that I would be an author, I didn't see it. In fact, I told Him I had nothing to write about and no story to share, and here we are where I've now had a lot to share. This became a new possibility. I want to encourage you to take some time to reflect on where you've been and where you've come from, and how you are no longer bound to certain things, and how in other areas you are taking it one day at a time with God. One thing for sure is that you may have a few thorns in your side, but when God comes into your life and begins to get all up in your business and begins healing, delivering, and fixing things, you're no longer able to be bound. Now you're processing through and daily walking out your freedom.

Prayer: Father, thank you for dwelling with me and coming into my heart and life invading every area, because where you are my freedom is found. Thank you for freeing me from the chains of bondage that have held me chained and bound for so long. Give me the ability to walk, talk, and be liberated in you. Father, thank you for taking the keys from the enemy to help me take back my life and regain my freedom. Thank you for keeping me in a place of vulnerability, letting you into the spaces that are even hard to address. Keep me humbled enough to find safe places that you send me to hold me accountable and keep me near you. Thank you for not letting me grow weary or frustrated with the things I feel are causing me to go in cycles, but let me lean more and press into you harder. Keep that thorn in my side and let me grow in you, and keep me guarded from the snares of the enemy. Let me continue to testify of what you've freed me from. Thank you for saving me from things that should've literally taken me out and kept me trapped. As I find my true freedom in you, help me to go back and take my sisters and everyone connected to me with me. Let me learn to be willing to fight for my freedom, their freedom, and my future generations' freedom. As I evolve and learn to walk out freedom, talk, and act like I'm a free, born-again woman, allow new opportunities, doors, relationships, and possibilities to present themselves, and let me walk in them if they're sent from you. Let freedom always be and remain my portion. Amen.

Vulnerable

"My grace is sufficient for you, for my power is made perfect in weakness. Therefore I will boast all the more gladly of my weaknesses, so that the power of Christ may rest upon me."–2 Corinthians 12:9 NIV

June 2017, my pastor did an altar call that completely changed the trajectory of my life. It was the day where I realized that vulnerability is the place of worship God wanted me to operate from. Prior to this experience and even a few times after, because it took some time still, I would go into God's presence hard hearted and guarded. I tried to keep Him at a distance and only allow Him to wreck my life how I wanted Him to. This altar call was going similar to that. In the beginning, I stood there a little detached yet longing for God to come in and speak to me, to do something in my heart and life, but what I didn't know was the missing ingredient was something that I was holding back from God, and that was me coming to him vulnerable and completed undone. He wanted me to lay down the cape that I thought I had to wear, walking around as if I was superwoman, handling all of my own problems and staying at my own rescue, and He wanted me to take off the mask that I had on hiding the tears and pain that I was feeling. Did I mention that He wanted the muzzle too? He made me open my mouth and speak to Him about what was bothering me and how I was really feeling. Yes, God sees and knows all, but that day I learned that He sometimes wants us to open our mouths and present that weakness to Him. Let me just say that when I broke at that altar that day, something unexplainable happened for me. I still till this day can't quite put it into words, but I reach times where I pray for God to take me back to that place and let me experience that plus some. That day I let God in wholeheartedly, and He came to see about me. I was no longer superwoman in His presence. I was Domonique, who was full of pain, scars, brokenness, and needed healing. I needed guidance, direction, and love. I got all of that, but it was only due to me accepting that role as being vulnerable. God's power is allowed to show up. God takes that same vulnerability that you allow when you are in His presence to take and use in your healing process by sharing your story and testimony with others, which heals you more and leads them to Him and their healing. I'd always joke about never liking crying and wanting to be so-called hard core, and during this book writing process alone, I've probably cried and become more vulnerable than ever, even sharing this experience with others during the journey, and now you. There's nothing pretty about getting into God's presence. It requires some messiness and ugliness getting to the vulnerable places, journeying to healing.

Prayer: Father, thank you for removing the walls of my heart that I've put up to block you and others out. Forgive me for being prideful entering into your presence as superwoman, trying to come as if I'm all that and well put together, when in actuality I'm broken, hurt, bruised, and scarred from things. Help me to practice coming to you undone, unfiltered, and vulnerable, allowing your perfection to show up in every weakness that I have. Thank you for loving me so much that you don't run from my brokenness but love me through it and heal every area. Remind me to be me when I'm with you. Thank you for reminders that you see and know all beyond what I portray. Continue to allow healing to be my portion and wholeness to be my story. Let me walk in constant relationship with you, and teach me to not run when I'm wrong and living in rebellion and sin, but to allow you in my life even at those times as well. Teach me how to navigate this relationship with you through vulnerability. I give you every piece of me and invite you into every room of my heart and life, especially the messy and ugly ones. Use it all for your glory and allow me to be a living proof of healing so that others will learn to come into your presence undone. No masks, no makeup, or no filters can ever replace what we have, and I thank you for that. Amen.

Worshipper

"God is a spirit and they that worship Him must worship Him in spirit and in truth." –John 4:24 KJV

If you're like me, you may be one who associated worship with music and what you offer God during the first 20-30 minutes of church. You may picture the praise dancers, mimes, choir, or even instrumentalists playing the beautiful slow songs, but let me help free you from that. While this is an act of worship that our Father loves, He is concerned about the posture of our hearts in everything that we do, moreso the things that we don't have words or language for, but our actions. God revealed to me how my whole life is an act of sacrifice and worship. God gave me breath in my lungs, activity in my limbs, and the ability to hear and understand everything that He wants me to do and when He wants me to do it. Your life and the way that you submit and surrender to the Father speaks volumes. You become a true worshipper when you are able to lift your hands and praise Him in the midst of adversity. Pray for a person who has persecuted you, slandered your name, or even treated you unfairly. How well can you love them? Being able to sow a seed when you're down to your last dime, yet still holding on to your faith and being able to trust God and praise Him in the midst. Many of you reading this may have experienced these moments like myself, and I want to encourage you that you have become a true worshipper, learning to stay planted and still glorify God and exalt Him in the midst, laying yourself aside for others. Your life and the way you live it, your words, thoughts, and actions have become your worship and make the difference in your worship time.

Prayer: Father, I pray for a heart after you show me how to worship you in spirit and in truth. Season the words that come from me, allow my behaviors and actions to be graceful and acceptable in your presence and set an example for others. Show me what's in me that's not of you, give me guidance on the areas of my life that need correction that aren't honoring you. I worship you, I adore you, I exalt you, and I lift you up now, Father. When life tries to make me weary, help me to press through and always result to worship. Show me new ways to worship you and live a life full out and pleasing to you. Let me live with the mindset of everything I do being done for you and not for self, to please others, or even for revenge of others, but to worship you and help build the kingdom. Thank you for loving me at all times, even the times where I wasn't in a space to worship fully or not in alignment with your will. Thank you for loving even the tainted and flawed parts of me that wanted to worship you but couldn't fully. I rededicate myself and my life to you from this day forward. I want to live a life poured out for you, one that represents you and leads others to you. Amen.

Xylophone

"Praise Him with trumpet sound; praise Him with lute and harp! Praise Him with tambourine and dance; praise Him with strings and pipe! Praise Him with sounding cymbals; praise Him with loud clashing cymbals."–Psalms 150:3-5 ESV

Being in concert band and marching band, you begin to learn that every instrument holds a significant place and has value in the symphony. I always wanted to play the saxophone and have been drawn to the string instruments, as they were the ones to play the beautiful melodies that I loved to hear. While I am intrigued by them still and dearly love them, God showed me the other love I have for percussion instruments, and not for their loudness but for how diverse they are. The bass drums ranging from small to large, the quads, and even the xylophone and cymbals that many never really selected as a first-choice instrument. These kind of happened to be given by default, but again, they held so much significance in the songs that we played. There were seasonal sounds that we couldn't fully play without having the xylophone present. God showed me how we are similar to these instruments and must be ready at all times to chime in and play our part in the song, whether we are holding down the chords or playing the melody or even simply keeping tempo. You and I both must find the beat and pick up our instruments to play our part, but we must follow the conductor to know when He is cueing us in. If not, you come in too early or miss it and get delayed, throwing other things off. I've witnessed it firsthand, a song completely falling apart because of coming in at the wrong timing and missing the conductor's cue. It doesn't matter if you feel like you are that tuba, bass drum, flute, clarinet, saxophone, or violin; pick up your instrument, watch for the conductor's cue, and play your part with confidence. You are so necessary in this melody, and you make that song better. There's a song that I love where the singer states "a sound precedes a move of God." There is a sound that the earth needs that's going to come from you. This sound will resound throughout the earth and shake nations. No matter how big or small you may seem, you have impact, and when you sound off, when you get the cue, the world shall hear you and experience God's move through you.

Prayer: Father, thank you for giving me a part to play in this symphony. Let me hold my part whether it's in the forefront playing the melody or in the background holding the chords. Show me how significant even the smallest thing I do is and how much I make an impact for your kingdom. Teach me how to show up confident and make a sound that will shake foundations that will usher in a move of God wherever I go. God, let your glory and presence be made known through me. God, let me keep my gaze set on you to watch closely for your cues and allow you to be the conductor over my life. Let me not delay or miss my cue but play my part when you give me the go. Let the sound resound and let it follow the encore and standing ovation for your glory and for all to come to know you. Help me to teach those around me to listen and focus for the cue and how to release their sound. Let me not try to mimic the sound of others but make the sound you specifically gave me to release, not the watered down or altered version. Amen.

You

"I praise you because I am fearfully and wonderfully made; your works are wonderful, I know that full well."–Psalms 139: 14 NIV

Authentic, different, bold, courageous, beautiful, smart. Some of these words just simply describe who I am when I am being that undiluted, authentic version of myself that hasn't tried to change or conform to who and what others want me to be or think I am. The whole purpose of this book was to explain how God helped me to realize over time this one important word: **that I am me and you are you, and we are who God created us to be and shouldn't aim to be anything different, because if we do, we become a counterfeit, fraud, and fake version of who we are really to show up as in the world.** We then deprive the world of experiencing what it needs to experience through our existence when we change who He created us to be. The big picture that I pray that many of you have grasped throughout this book is that although the world we live in right now has on masks naturally and some in the spirit, it's time to remove the masks and unbecome to become everything that God wants us to be. It's time out for being anything but that. God wants us to show up and let the person He planned before the beginning of the earth finally arrive and emerge into her place. That may mean being you in style, personality, character, attitude, speech, creativity and more, because if we all were the same exact replica of one another, the world would be an absolutely boring place. We must no longer allow ourselves, the enemy, or others to make us believe that we need to change and alter our true self, especially when it aligns with who and what God says you are, to be something else. The day that I no longer walked around trying to take pieces of everyone else to make this perfect version of me was the day I became free in knowing that I can only be Domonique Shantel Peele, and the only person I want to be a replica of is Christ. I want to walk, talk, and be more like Him, but I can do that and be me at the same time. He already factored this in. I pray that you, too, will no longer waste another day trying to substitute the parts of you that the world needs or being the counterfeit. You're wasting valuable time. The world is waiting for you to show up unapologetic about your true being and be you.

Prayer: Father, first off, forgive me of my being vain and not appreciating the art of who you created me to be, thinking that I could create a better version of myself and not accepting who you've called me to be and who you created me to be and show up as in the earth. Where I lack knowledge of who I am in you, peel back the scales, heal the shattered, broken, and uncertain areas, even those parts of me that have allowed others to tell me who I am, even when it didn't align with your word. Forgive me for believing the lies more than I believed your word. Let this moment be the last moment that I waste another breath or bit of time playing small, diluting myself, or conforming to what others want me to be. Show me who you've called me to be and the ways you made me. Father, not only show me, but allow me to come into complete agreement with it and accept my truth, knowing that without me, someone in the world is missing out on the true version of me and possibly an encounter with you. Father, let me breathe in this truth, that I am who you created me to be, and I have the right, authority, and power to live out loud, to be bold, to be confident and not have to apologize for being me. Remind me when I forget, you knew every ounce of my life and who I'd be before I even existed, and you saw me as good and fit to be here, so allow me to show up and be. From this day forward, peel back the layers, remove the mask, and let me unbecome to become everything you want me to. I won't waste another day not being me or being free. Continue to send and show me who is for me, and those who aren't and don't receive me for me, help me to forgive them and move forward, not harboring offense or allowing myself to dwell on the why's and why not's of how they didn't accept me. Amen.

Zesty

"You are the salt of the earth, but if the salt has lost its taste, how shall its saltiness be made salty again? It is no longer good for anything, except to be thrown out and trampled underfoot. You are the light of the world. A town built on a hill cannot be hidden."–Matthew 5:13-14 NIV

In other words, you're the "It factor." You bring the sizzle, the razzle dazzle. When you come in, some things must change, atmospheres must shift. You don't have to conform or change to fit the room. Why? Because you were created to stand out, not to fit in or be hidden. There's something in you that the world needs to see. When you step foot into the room, all darkness must flee because your light outshines it. Your light overpowers anything that ever existed prior to you stepping foot in that room. Once you stepped in, the devil and his posse had to or has to flee. There will be times God places you in rooms where you may not understand how you got there or even how you fit in there, and you'll eventually realize that there was a specific reason for Him sending you there or strategically placing you there. He needed you to add your spice to the room and give them a splash of Jesus. One thing that I found growing up is that it was easier to conform to the standards of the world and shrink back on my whole radical "Jesus girl" stance, because comfort felt better, acceptance felt better, the background felt better, being silent seemed like the better option. I didn't want to seem like a sore thumb sticking out. I didn't want to be the outcast in the room. What I really didn't realize was that I was falling victim to the enemy's tricks to change my posture, to change my heart, to change my mindset, and to take me from a place of authority to one of conformity and comfort. While work was going undone because I was afraid to speak and allow God to use my seasoned speech to heal someone's heart or lead them to Him. I refused to praise and the enemy was being exalted more than God in that moment because I wouldn't lift up a praise to my Heavenly Father. I was shifting my standards rather than upholding my convictions from Holy Spirit. I've learned over time to take back my confidence in who I was and what I had to offer to the world. While the world as a whole may not come to know Domonique Shantel Peele on a personal level, those that I do come into contact with will catch a dose of this sugar, spice, and everything nice that God has gifted me with. I've learned to walk more confidently and boldly into rooms and play my part well so that those I come into contact with will come to know Him, if nothing else. I vowed that no one would leave my presence without a sprinkle of Jesus and the taste of His goodness left with them. You, too, have to begin to walk in the room as if you know that God has given you something special to offer, something unique that can't be found anywhere else, something with a special gracing on it. It's time to let your light shine and your salt to overshadow some things.

160

www.ingramcontent.com/pod-product-compliance
Lightning Source LLC
Chambersburg PA
CBHW051103160426
43193CB00010B/1294